sex& the single parent

A Guide for Parents Who Find
Themselves Back in the Dating Game

Most Perigee Books are available at special quantity discounts for bulk purchases for sales promotions, premiums, fund-raising, or educational use. Special books, or book excerpts, can also be created to fit specific needs.

For details, write: Special Markets, The Berkley Publishing Group, 375 Hudson Street, New York, New York 10014.

sex & the single parent

A Guide for Parents Who Find
Themselves Back in the Dating Game

Meg F. Schneider, M.S.W., and
Martine J. Byer, C.S.W.

A Perigee Book

A Perigee Book
Published by The Berkley Publishing Group
A division of Penguin Putnam Inc.
375 Hudson Street
New York, New York 10014

First edition: November 2002

Visit our website at www.penguinputnam.com

Library of Congress Cataloging-in-Publication Data

Schneider, Meg F.
    Sex & the single parent : a guide for parents who find themselves back in the
dating game / Meg F. Schneider and Martine J. Byer.—1st ed.
        p. cm.
    ISBN 0-399-52820-2
    1. Single parents—Social life and customs. 2. Divorced parents—Social life and
customs. 3. Dating (Social customs). 4. Man-woman relationships. 5. Parent and
child. I. Title: Sex and the single parent. II. Byer, Martine J. III. Title.

HQ759.915 .S35 2002
306.85'6—dc21
                                                                            2002029312

Printed in the United States of America

10 9 8 7 6 5 4 3 2 1

To Adam and Jason, who think I'm a better mother when I'm dating.

—MFS

To Laurel, the child I cherish and will love forever, who shares with me endlessly interesting, surprising, and precious moments that make my life so much more.

—MJB

Contents

Introduction:

What Do We Need Him for, or Can I Come Too?

> You're single again. It's 7 P.M., the sitter has arrived, and you have a date. It's your third night out with this man and it's for dinner at a lovely restaurant. Third dates, you know, or at least have been told, are the deal makers or breakers. You look in the mirror turning from side to side. You look good—even a little glamorous. Feeling a little anxious you walk into the living room just as the doorbell rings. Teddy, your eight-year-old son, bolts for the door.
>
> "Who is it?" he sings out.
>
> You can actually hear the hesitation on the other side of the door. You look through the peephole. It's Sam.
>
> You open the door, Sam walks in, your son takes one look at him and says with a notable amount of disgust, "Oh. Your boyfriend is here."

Dating in front of the children, is, among other things, a crowded experience. It's difficult enough for two adults with complicated lives and an abundance of responsibilities—not to mention fears—to get to know each other. Add to this the demanding, needy, and ofttimes interfering presence of children, and the landscape becomes even more complex.

Sex and the Single Parent is the first and only guide you will need to navigate the complicated dynamics that occur when single parents begin "courting," form relationships, and become ensconced in long-term partnerships.

It is a book for both men and women who find themselves in the dating game for the first time in possibly ten, fifteen, or twenty years. Through the use of real-life scenarios as well as insightful straightforward narrative this book will not only explore key issues but also offer extensive "hands-on" assistance.

What do you say to a six-year-old who pitches a fit every time you walk out the door with a date? How do you explain to your ten-year-old that on *this* vacation you will be sharing a room with your boyfriend and she and her sister can have their own room? What do you do when your teenage daughter tells you to "button up your blouse? What is this? A bordello?"

You will have many conflicting emotions as you try to move through these highly complex (and sometimes enraging and embarrassing) moments. You may sometimes want to close your eyes and cover your ears. But you really can't. You have to deal with your feelings as well as those of your children. This is especially true when your needs are most polarized. There is a balance that has to be reached that respects your natural need for emotional and physical connections but also takes into account your children's ages, their sense of loss and fear of abandonment, and their natural desire to stay close to you.

That is what this book is about.

Sex and the Single Parent explores how to balance your need to date up against your children's, at best, confusion, and at worst, complete resistance. This resistance can come in all forms, varying intensity and enduring for short or long periods of time. Patience is key.

But sooner or later all of you will be able to move forward not by walking tentatively through a minefield, but by feeling understood and learning to embrace the wonderful changes life can bring.

Throughout this book you will find a multitude of scenarios that are very common to the single parent who is trying to create a personal life with children always in the picture. These anecdotes have sprung from interviews and clients who generously shared their "fingernail across the blackboard" experiences. If you've just started dating you'll have a major head start on handling the dynamics that are sure to surface. If you have been dating awhile you may or may not find the exact scene that has played out in your life but chances are you will find something similar to help you when those basic dynamics repeat themselves. You might even be able to use some advice to undo a bit of damage that's already been done. (What parent in retrospect wishes they hadn't said "*that*"!) In most cases we have tried to explore not only how you would handle the situation for the particular aged child involved, but also what you might have done if that child were younger or older.

No matter how you became a single parent this book is meant to empower you to search for what you need while at the same time tending to the concerns of your children.

You have a right to the companionship you seek and the love you need.

Your children have a right to have their concerns, fears, and questions addressed and their feelings of loss attended to.

And all of you, together, need to embrace the fact that a new person, while disruptive at first to the status quo, and hard to get used to as the months tick by, and according to your children "sometimes in the way," can in fact be a boon. And not just eventually. Handled with sensitivity your dates, almost from the beginning, can add something very positive to everyone's outlook on life.

Who better than you to model that a quest for loving companionship is a good thing? And if and when you find that love, who better to prove to your children that one can weather the most emotionally trying storms and come out stronger, happier, and wiser?

This book is about building your new personal life. But it is also about helping your children grow into optimistic people who understand that change isn't just about loss, and that love is still something in which to believe.

1

Do I Still Have It?

MARYANNE sat and stared at the face on her computer screen. His screen name was PERFECT4YOU. She sighed. Maybe for someone, but not for her. Maryanne clicked for her next "match." She had been at this computer dating for months. It was better than dances. The thought of them made her sick. It was better than bars. Walking into a crowded restaurant and sitting by herself on a stool waiting for some reasonably attractive guy to find her reasonably attractive in turn, made her skin crawl. So here she sat, in the privacy of her own home. With both kids in bed, she was quietly doing her thing. Or so she thought.

"What are you doing, Mom?" A voice from behind her suddenly rang through the air.

Maryanne started and whirled around to find her thirteen-year-old son staring at the screen, which now held a vertical row of three one-inch-by-one-inch male faces.

"Who's that?" he continued, moving closer. He was squinting.

"Nothing!" she practically yelped clicking the exit button as quickly as she could manage. "How come you're not asleep?!"

She glared at her son, who stood rooted to the spot. "I just wanted to ask you something. . . ." he said meekly. He was clearly confused. "What's wrong?"

Maryanne looked away with shame. Embarrassment. Confusion.

How had she arrived at a place where her adolescent son was actually watching her hunt for a man at the very time he was starting to check out girls?

How had her life gotten so . . . pathetic?

It Wasn't Supposed to Be This Way

Once, you had a partner. Fallling in love and feeling so right with another person was one of life's sweetest offerings. You reveled in the warmth of having found that person with whom you could explore the world, have children, and spend the rest of your life.

But somehow it started to sour. You tried to fix it. You went to marriage counseling, talked to friends and relatives, tried romantic vacations, bought each other peace offerings, once, twice, too many times. You wanted to make it work. Who wanted to be single again? Who wanted to parent alone? But to no avail.

So after many false fresh starts with your partner you decided (both decided) that you could not take this ride together anymore.

Or perhaps you are a widow or widower. Or maybe you only had a live-in lover but it was a long and serious relationship, and now he's gone. Perhaps you were suddenly, horribly, abandoned by your mate.

Whatever your previous situation, you are now alone. With the children.

You are scared, liberated, perplexed, excited, and worried. You are loaded with responsibilities and pressures you've never had before. This is new terrain.

Being single is not exactly entirely foreign. You've been single before. You somewhat enjoyed (okay, never that much) the rounds of dating, and eyeing potential romantic possibilities on planes and trains. You've scouted out at health clubs and at parties, attended concerts (always with binoculars) and plays. You've roamed the supermarket aisles with one eye on the produce and another on the person just diagonally to the right. Yes, you've done that. And when it was over, and you were attached to someone, you thought, "Well, thank god for that. The search is over. I am single no more." Now not only are you single again, but you are single with children.

And you have major responsibility for your children. So it often happens that, the responsible for children part eclipses the single adult part. There's so much you have to do for them and so little time for yourself. Sure, you have romantic, sexual, emotional needs. But you can no longer fill them with only yourself in mind.

What you do about your social life is no longer only your business. Decisions can't be made now on whims. Spontaneity is simply not a word in your vocabulary . . . or in most cases, not on weekdays and two weekends out of the month.

Where in My Adult World Do I Belong?

A new phase of your life has begun. A great deal will continue on as it always has; your friends will be there (except for the ones who find the divorce threatening or feel a greater loyalty to your ex). Your sister and your parents will still love you (though maybe they judge you just a tad too much). But something will change. When you are not invited to the theater with two of your couple friends, you are genuinely hurt. "Well, it was always the six of us," Judy explains. "I'm so sorry, it's just that I figured you wouldn't really want to come on your own and I didn't know how to bring it up."

Maybe she's right. Being the fifth wheel could have been awkward for you. Still, you've been left out and that feels bad. A woman you trust gets weird and acts as if you are making a play for her husband. You're not even attracted to him. He's just old

Jimmy; you've known him for years. Some of your friends drop away, creating more loss, another blow.

It finally hits you—you are not going to fit in the way you once did. When your children are not with you, you are alone. Days and nights spent wrapped in family details are now wide-open spaces. Even when the kids are with you, you have no adult with whom to bounce off ideas. You may feel walled in by your child's world and experience an extreme loss of freedom. Where once there was a partner to provide a break, you are now completely dependent on baby-sitters (who aren't always available) or relatives (who resent giving the time). The awesome responsibility of your child just grows bigger, higher, and wider.

But take a breath and be patient. Slowly you will see that the changes you are experiencing, though dramatic and sometimes unpleasant, are creating the road for rewarding changes. Life can be good. You can create a place for yourself, and although it may take longer than you'd like, you have a chance to discover so many important things about yourself—wonderful things you might have missed if you'd stayed married. . . .

Who Am I Most Now? A Parent or Lover?

"Do you have to have a man to be happy?" many of your dearest friends may ask, as they prepare dinner for their husbands, or wait for him to call to say what time he'll be home. ". . . To feel complete?" some may add, for extra nauseating measure.

You'll likely want to slap them. The truth is for you the answer may be "yes," but not the way they mean it. You might like yourself a lot. You might feel extremely successful, clever, and loving. You enjoy your girlfriends tremendously and love being a mother. But, yes. You might also feel that you need a sexual and romantic relationship. You might want a loving and supportive bond with a member of the opposite sex in order to feel fulfilled. Understood. Desired.

Your friends may ask this question because they're exhausted with their own relationships, tired of your unhappiness, or simply completely out of touch with what it means to be alone . . . no less alone with the demands single parenting adds to the mix. So no matter how you answer them, don't be afraid to say, at least to yourself, "You're darn right. I want a companion. A lover. I like myself and I want someone to see why."

No matter how you look at it, healthy adult love is different than the love of a child or the love for work and friends. Each love relationship has its own particular elements that meet specific needs. Children can satisfy your maternal self. You can get invaluable sustenance from a friend. But there is much you can receive from a partner that you simply can't get from other places. Most people want partner love in their lives and that's a good thing; it does not indicate a problem.

Of course you want to date. The problem is it requires that you wear two hats and for the most part, at the exact same time. Although this was true within a marriage, you were not doing so under the watchful (suspicious, curious, angry, scared, loving confused) eyes of your offspring.

Perhaps the biggest truth of your dual role is this:

On balance, your role of parent has to come first . . . no matter what.

LAURIE had a night out. Her mother was with the children and she felt as free as a bird. She left the office, did a quick workout, and after showering, felt refreshed enough to join some coworkers at a restaurant. Unexpectedly she found herself attracted to the office manager's brother who just happened to come along. Lucky break. He had just transferred jobs and his sister was introducing him around. Laurie sat, laughing and talking about the places she'd traveled, and noticed there seemed to be a genuine connection between them. The gods were smiling upon her.

Then her cell phone rang. Jill, her seven-year-old, was sick and crying for her. She was running a fever of 103 degrees. Okay, Laurie thought to herself. It's high but kids run high fevers. Do I have to run home? I left her with a capable adult, I'm a good mother, she's in good hands. But she's crying. Laurie turned to look at her companion. Everything had changed. The tone, the energy, the electricity had gone. He knew it. He could see it in her face. She knew it. She could feel it in every cell of her body.

She had to go home.

It had been going so well. She'd felt alive and sexual. The door to her domestic home life had closed briefly and it had been glorious. Now it had to be opened to Jill's crying from what turned out to be a major case of strep.

An hour later Laurie found herself in her kitchen on the phone talking to doctors and mashing Tylenol into vanilla fudge ice cream. Jill would have never taken this concoction from anyone else but her. Laurie knew it was good that she had come home quickly.

But good for whom?

"What about me?" she found herself thinking. "When will it ever be time for me to have me again?" And then that thought crept in. The one no single parent ever wants to lay claim to. The one that comes in a flash and disappears just as quickly . . . not just because of guilt but because the thought, while intoxicating (liberating?), is also intolerable.

"I sometimes wish that I had no children."

The Crux of the Conflict

When it comes right down to it, sometimes your kids are and will continue to be in your romantic way. Acknowledging that thought can be upsetting and guilt provoking. After all, aren't they also your greatest gift?

The answer is yes, but why must you condemn yourself to want only one gift? Why can't you allow yourself to relax with the idea that a parent is not all you are and that you naturally need other kinds of emotional sustenance? Feeling that you need to hide from your wish to leave your kids and run off to explore the world can be deadly for everyone. Your frustrations and unhappiness will seep out in some other way. Difficult feelings of anger, resentment, and frustration are normal. Guilt is normal too; it comes with the parenting territory of any type of parenting and especially single parenting. As a single parent, you may have a tendency to want to compensate for the child's loss of the ideal togetherness that came in the shape of two loving parents at home. But you can't. The fact is your children will be far better able to cope with this loss with honest emotions if you deal forthrightly with your own. They will pick up on your efforts to hide from those dark and painful thoughts and wonder what's going on. They may feel frightened. Insecure. They may start to feel as if they cannot trust you. But if you directly face these feelings either with a friend, relative, or therapist, if you bring them into the light of day, what you do bring home, in terms of your body language, or temper or tone of voice, will be less laden with negative vibrations.

You can be a capable, loving parent and an adult who listens to and meets your own intimacy needs. Of course pulling this off does require all sorts of maturity that can be hard to muster up in the aftermath of a crisis. However, the road to glory is paved with getting honest about your fears and concerns. And let's face it. Those fears and concerns aren't simply about being a successful parent while conducting a torrid love affair.

Will Anyone Want Me?

Once you have healed sufficiently to face your life with its new reality, things may be looking more complicated than you could have imagined. A yearned-for lover may not appear easily. Aside from your children, you carry with yourself a complicated history and a morass of hurts and insecurities that can make finding a partner seem terrifying if not impossible.

You may have been with the same guy for years. He's seen you in all manner of disrepair. During the good times you were an object of his desire, a beauty, and as sexy as you could possibly be.

You had been passionate about each other much of the time, and when you weren't, you certainly could get in the mood quickly enough. Yes, toward the end there was nothing there but that was because the relationship had gone astray. But was it the end of the relationship that cooled his ardor or did you become less attractive and kill the relationship?

You are older than when you first stripped with abandon (or at least with only moderate anxiety) and may be thinking to yourself, "Can I still get steamy?"

Can I Still Attract the Opposite Sex?

A year after the marriage was over, Jane was finally ready to date. As she stood in front of her dresser mirror she saw that she was pretty. Her chestnut hair was shiny and worn in a style that complimented her face. Seeing herself, as if through someone else's eyes, she looked good so far. Then she stripped to her underwear and stood in front of the full-length mirror. She first tried to get a view from her best side, her most flattering angle. It used to be good, really good. She inspected herself with a critical eye. After two kids and eleven years she thought, not bad, not the same but still reasonable. Unfortunately these are things for which a new guy might not make allowances. After all, he hadn't known her in the unstoppable, tight-as-a-drum years. Someone new will only see her as she is now, not as she was.

It can be tremendously difficult to hang on to a view of yourself as a sexy, alluring adult. It can seem almost silly . . . as if who do you think you're kidding? The truth is you're kidding no one. People can retain their sexiness, their ability to attract the opposite sex without trying.

When you're young and strutting like a little peacock in sleek jeans, or floating along in a blue velvet dress, you emphasize the external and count on being eye-catching. But years bring wisdom, and if you allow yourself, you can see, and even feel, how true attraction really isn't only skin-deep.

Anne sat in her living room with her brother and sister-in-law gazing at a picture of herself, taken when she was nineteen years old. "I was great-looking then," she said aloud with a heavy sigh, keenly feeling the loss. "I think you look better now actually," her sister-in-law piped up. "You were a lot . . . I don't know . . . tougher-looking then?" She hesitated, gazing at Anne thoughtfully. "You're softer-looking now. It's lovely. Maybe it's an inner thing. . . ."

An inner thing? Take it. As you gain experience, you radiate a range of feelings from an internal place that does have its own wonderful set of external alluring properties as well.

Am I Interesting Enough?

Roger is forty-two and shy. He met his first wife in a library when they were both graduate students in literature. They connected over William Blake and went into a marital trance for twelve years and three daughters. They made a cocoon together and left their old worlds behind. After his wife announced she wanted out, Roger finally came to, and found that he hadn't really developed as a person at all. His head had been in books and the routine grind of family life: diapers, kid movies, bath times, piano, dance and music recitals. He had been showing up, reciting his lines, and allowing the play to unfold. Now that he is back in the dating pool Roger fears that women will find him narrow and dull. He is scared to try to connect to someone new because he doesn't know how. He doesn't know what to talk about—it's been so long since something other than the routine demands of his life has grabbed his attention.

Roger needs to step back into his learning curve. It's common for a long-term relationship to put a lid on many areas of emotional development. Couples make agreements. You are the one who is good at providing and I'm the one who is good at planning our social life. While this may be true, it also closes down each partner to exploring, growing, and becoming stronger in other areas. For example, it is hard for a kid to learn to clean his room and organize himself when a parent moves in very quickly to do it for him. If a challenge can be met easily by your partner (or parent) then you don't have to take it on yourself. Now that Roger's life is wide open and he is solo, he has a new opportunity to find strengths and skills that he will need on this leg of the journey. He's tense and scared—anyone would be—but this life change could bring him discovery and a new level of personal confidence. Crisis is opportunity.

Will I Ever Trust Again?

Teri is lonely. The divorce absolutely broadsided her. When her husband came home and said he was leaving, it was a classic out-of-the-blue scenario. She was a good wife. Or at least she thought she was. They'd just returned from a lovely vacation two weeks before the shocking announcement. Sure, Bill had seemed somewhat distant. But he got like that occasionally. Teri is haunted by her own misperceptions and her ex's abandonment. How can she really ever be sure of herself or anyone else again?

When you're in a marriage and particularly in a long one, you build most of your world around another person. Rules and agreements made early as well as those that develop along the way, whether openly and silently observed, may be followed faithfully by one person and viewed as "flexible" by the other. As things change they are not discussed and so when reality hits, the loss, the betrayal of vows is shattering.

As Teri examines the world she thought she was living in with Bill, she found that there were clues of her husband's unhappiness that she allowed to slip by unattended. In taking stock and reflecting on this landscape, Teri will learn to assert herself. This will give her understanding and power over her own feelings and allow her to trust that she can take care of herself again.

A betrayal is one painful way to learn the importance of being open to the many messages that come our way. Teri no doubt, within her marriage, missed positive messages as well. Once you gain confidence in your ability to know what's going on around you it's possible you will be more aware of not just the negative moments but also become more exquisitely attuned to the positive!

What If I'm Alone Forever?

After the decision was made and her husband moved out, Jennifer did not waste any time. When her son was with his father, she was out at clubs, lectures, movies, and on blind dates. She still had it, the old charm, the social skill to catch a man's eye and strike up a conversation. Every available minute was absorbed with searching for and being in some kind of connection. The guys—some nice, some okay, some a drag—were great distractions, even entertaining, but not a great love match was among them. Jennifer found that with her good looks and smartness intact, it was still hard to find that deep and special feeling with someone she craved. "Where is he?" Jennifer asks herself practically every night. She's frustrated and scared that she could end up alone forever.

Beginning the quest for a new love can be exciting and after a while daunting. There are many variables in making a good match and getting them all in one person can seem impossible sometimes. The truth is that no one knows exactly when that connection will come along again, and people naturally get scared that it won't . . . especially when a bout of loneliness sets in. It's fine to project a year ahead and say things will be different, and it's quite another to have to get through the next five days with pressures and responsibilities when there is no one there with whom to share them or from whom to get a soft, comforting touch. The wait can seem limitless. When the need for a companion is high and hot, it is hard to have faith. It's important to interrupt and skim off the pessimism whenever you have the strength to do so. Replace a doomed thought with a positive one.

Be Careful What You Wish For . . .
Be Realistic

There will come a time when you meet someone with whom you can have a brief but lovely romance or a truly meaningful relationship. Undoubtedly it will feel wonderful. Of course the context within which this relationship plays itself out will be unlike anything else you have ever experienced. You have kids, you have an ex, and you now have a very complicated life to keep in balance. Finding companionship is worth the trials it might inspire, but it's a good idea to be aware that what you most wish for can underline the problems you already have and inspire new ones as well. Reality is going to be tricky.

Exes Forever

He hears you got a raise or a boyfriend and he starts trying to renegotiate the financial agreement. Or, he has a habit of canceling at the last minute and not picking up the kids until hours after he promised. Your date is left waiting . . . until you have to cancel altogether. Or she decides to take advantage of her custodial parent status, and keep the kids from enjoying a day with you and your date's children. Everyone is thrown off balance. He's there always. She's there always. Your ex is a constant reminder that life didn't mimic *The Donna Reed Show*. In some ways you feel as if you are going to have to pay for this fact forever.

He Can't Be Everything *He* Wasn't

This time, you've told yourself, you're going to get it right. That's fine. But you'll need to keep in mind that no one gets it perfect. You can't right everything wrong with your ex. Your new partner can't fix what happened, or bring you no problems of his or her own. The issues are different but hopefully they will be more attuned with your own. Perhaps your personality is better matched for his needs than those of your ex. But he may disappoint you.

She may tick you off. There is no problem-free relationship. Sometimes even adults seem to forget this. They've been through so many problems that they imagine *next* time things will be great. And they may be. But not perfectly great.

You Can't Please All of the People All of the Time

Your girlfriend expects to spend her birthday with you. Your kids want to see the latest movie on the same night and it's your scheduled time with them. Your boyfriend has planned a beautiful evening on his sailboat for the two of you. Suddenly your son hands you a school flyer he'd forgotten to fork over two weeks ago. It's parent-teacher night. The moon and the waves are going to have to wait. The question is, will your boyfriend?

Scheduling Spontaneity

You manage to have some time together with your boyfriend, but there's pressure to make it great. The days of lazy weekends where one hour can melt into another at whim are in the past and may not appear in your future. You can't relax and let whatever happen, good or bad.

But you can take advantage of the time you can steal away for yourselves. You can put a little extra effort into thinking how you can make it special, exciting, maybe electric! It's not going to happen at the spur of the moment. Planned excitement sounds like a contradiction in terms but it doesn't have to be.

Barbara found dating made her absolutely crazy. She'd rush home from her teaching job, get dinner on the table for James and Annie, and then race to get dolled up for an alluring look, while she actually felt totally depleted. She was doing it all to make a movie schedule or dinner reservation. She discovered that trying to get psyched for the date while also trying to be there for the kids, whose needs were unpredictable, was near to impossible. She found herself resenting everyone. Finally Barbara suggested to Tom that on baby-sitter night, they do something casual without having to meet at a specific time. She would call him when she was ready. They began to take walks along the river. In cold weather they dined at simple neighborhood places. She found she arrived less hassled, more relaxed, and most importantly able to be present. It wasn't perfect but it was so much better.

Finally, Still Not Alone

So the kids are both finally teenagers. In fact one is off to college. Finally it's time to relax as there is not much reason to hide anything anymore. Right? Wrong? Fifteen-year-olds, eighteen-year-olds, and twenty-year-olds can still be children. They may still wish you'd never split. They may feel competitive with your social life. They may feel as if they simply don't want you to have a life of your own. Not yet. Not ever. Or they may be perfectly happy for you to have one but their problems (which all kids have) are your problems as well.

Finally, there is your child's-eye view. You've gotten a grip on forming a new life, you have some sense of your enduring attractiveness, you realize romance has to happen in a whole new way, and you realize you can't fix the past by creating a perfect present. You're centered.

But are your children? What does all this look like to them? You'd probably love not having to worry about this but their perceptions are your problems.

"You're Going Out Again?"

After the trauma of divorce you are especially pressured to do right by your children. You will want to ease the transition and insure they get their emotional balance back. You will want to help them feel secure, be confident in your love and attention, and see them greet the world with a positive attitude despite the disruption in their lives.

You will also want them to let you date without causing any problems.

This isn't going to happen and it isn't their fault. Of course it isn't yours either but it is your responsibility (that word is probably becoming anathema to you) to make sure your personal life does not debilitate them in any way.

"Why Do You Have to Go Out?"

This is the frequent battle cry of young children who are particularly out to lunch when it comes to what you might need in your life. "Why can't I come?" is another refrain that can occur as you are combing your hair and touching up your mascara for a night out. It's not easy to explain that some other need is greater this evening than their need to be with you. If they are well and have a nice baby-sitter you will have to combat your own unreasonable guilt and their unreasonable demands. By the time you walk out the door you might be too exhausted for the date. But as time goes by you'll be able to handle this conflict with more equilibrium.

"She's Weird. Why'd You Pick Her?"

You meet someone you really like. She charms you at the theater, concerts, picks interesting places for dinner, and gets along nicely with your friends. They think she might be a keeper. After two months you introduce your school-age children to her. Immediately come the tests. Poor behavior, rude conversation, and intolerable attempts to come between you. Telling them to stop may make a difference for about five minutes. You had started the evening as a suave gentleman and now you're just short of becoming a raving lunatic. For some reason your children are determined to keep your girlfriend out, and from the look on her face they are doing a simply marvelous job. Did you mess up the timing on the introductions? If you had waited years (like twenty) or done it sooner (in an earlier life) it might have turned out better. Or maybe not? Maybe not at all? Maybe another partner will never be "right."

And does that have to matter?

"Oh Mom. I Liked Him!"

You take your sons and a man you've been dating to a great baseball game. It turns out to be a very happy event. The boys really like Jim. And you like Jim so it seems fine for now. The boys ask about Jim. They want to know if he has children, what he does for work, and what other sports he's into. Jim is also taken with your children, which is great.

The only problem is while you like Jim a lot, as time has gone by you like him incrementally less. In fact, your boys like Jim more than you do. Now what?

FOR better (not worse) your new life has begun. You are at first tentative but then increasingly more ready to find a companion for this next part of life's ride. Your children are included whether they want to be or not. Whether at times you want them around or not. A balance needs to be found. You need to be satisfied and your children supported. Your new partner needs attention and you. Sometimes you may feel as if you are being torn apart by a team of wild horses.

You are.

But you can tame them all, once you achieve an inner balance. By understanding your needs and those of your children you will find that the right compromise comes naturally, easily, and comfortably. You can be a lover and a mother. You can be a wonderful father and an attentive boyfriend. But you can't do it torn apart inside by guilt or uncertainty. You can only do it if deep inside you can trust yourself to make the right decisions *most* of the time—to know who needs you how much, when and why; and where you really need to be.

The place to begin is with yourself. One of the most complex tasks in any relationship is being clear on where your boundaries are. Knowing where you begin and end and what strengths and limitations you have is key. Communicating authentically to your children is vital especially after a profound change that has altered their worlds and yours as all of you have known it.

Beyond that there is one other issue that this complex world presents the single woman in particular. And that is keeping yourself and your children safe.

Conducting a Safe Search

The world is your dating pool. A church gathering, a temple dance, a singles organization dinner, the personals. The list is plentiful . . . offering endless possibilities of meeting not only just a prince but a rather dangerous frog. Who are these people you are meeting, these people no one you know has introduced you to? How safe are you in letting them take a step into you and your children's lives?

Busy people, and this is exponentially true for single parents, are turning more and more to online dating services where little color photos accompanying somewhat exaggerated bios are accessed by the simple touch of a button. Suddenly possibilities are scrolling across your screen: doctors, lawyers, and chefs. Direct marketing consultants and self-employed financiers. In a dry spell online dating can remind you there are other single people out there, who are lonely and searching. It's not a bad thing to know.

The only thing is you have to keep in mind they may also be lying.

And not just about their looks, or religion, or height, or age. They may simply be "players" who hop from picture to date to picture to date looking for a score. These meetings with no real context require a solid and clearheaded approach. You want to explore. And so you should. But you must proceed cautiously, for your own safety, as well as that of your kids. Who is this man who has come from cyberspace? Should he really know your address so quickly? The place where your children live? Maybe so. Maybe not.

Jollie walked in the door Friday evening, completely annoyed because the man she was supposed to have met at a lovely bar a few towns over never appeared. No sooner had she taken off her coat when Todd, her thirteen-year-old son came bolting down the stairs, eyes wide, voice shaking.

"Mom, where were you?!" he cried out.

She looked at him mystified. She went out on dates quite often. She wasn't even late. "Getting stood up!" she said with a little laugh. But then she paused. Her son looked almost out of control. "Honey, what is it?" she asked reaching for him with both arms.

"Some guy called and wanted to know where you were. He said he'd been waiting and waiting and maybe you'd been hit by a truck or something!"

Don't give out your number so fast. Listen to how he talks about his children. If things are going well, after a short time, introduce him to friends. There's no point in rushing a good thing, and everything to gain from finding out in a safe way if it's a bad thing.

But even aside from your physical self it's important to protect your emotional self as well. Countless articles have been written on the false intimacy a barrage of e-mails can create. A great picture, some witty exchanges, then some deeper e-mail confessions, leading to a great phone conversation and many people feel as if they are already falling in love. They aren't. Or rather perhaps they are but they're enamored by a fantasy.

This is not to say that online dating can never find you the perfect mate. Rather it's to say you could never possibly know that before getting to know each other up close and personal.

Above All, Keep Your Sense of Humor, While Crying

Though Jenny had originally abhorred blind dates, she chanced them now and then. So far they hadn't been too bad, though none had been quite right. Each time she reached home, paid the sitter, and kissed her sleeping children, she'd think, "What a waste. I should have stayed home with my kids and spent the money on a new lace bra. Then again, who's going to see it?" It was this frustration that allowed her to accept the offer made by a friend to give her number to Scott.

On Thursday at seven, she answered her door and there he was. Physically, he wasn't her type but she reminded herself a person can grow on another person. Still she had to push away that pit of the stomach sinking feeling of disappointment. The pinkie ring didn't help either. She'd always had a bad association with men and jewelry.

He was a nice guy, noticing and complimenting her on some photos she had taken that were hanging on the wall. He'd chosen a lovely restaurant for dinner. As they walked out on to the street, Jenny had talked herself into being more comfortable. Then Scott turned to her and asked in quite a serious tone, "Jenny, do you like chicken?" "Yes," she replied. "Why do you ask?"

Scott positioned his elbow in a triangular shape, holding his hand on his hip and said (after giving a chicken cluck or two) "Good, so grab a wing." Jenny's jaw dropped. It struck her as so dumb and corny she could hardly bear it. She didn't know whether to laugh or cry or go screaming down the street in the other direction. Her eight-year-old had more wit than Scott.

"He was just trying to be nice," her sister said the next day.

"But a chicken wing?" Jenny pulled the covers over her head and willed herself into a nap before her daughter returned. "I don't have the strength for her," Jenny thought to herself. I feel too sad and disappointed.

* * *

JUGGLING every aspect of your life to make room for a social/ romantic life is taxing, exciting, and sometimes funny. It can also leave you feeling frustrated, pathetic, undesirable, and woefully depressed . . . and in no mood to handle your children's problems, demanding behaviors, and endless needs.

The trick is to keep going in a measured fashion. If you need to take a rest from the dating scene and spend some time with good friends, do it. A frenzied search for a mate rarely ends well. A well-paced and balanced active life in which you remain emotionally open to whomever might come along should be your goal. There's a lot on your plate. Ironically you can feel very boxed in just at the time when you would like to be expansive. Experiment. Be free.

2

Parenting and Dating: Who's More Important? Him or Me?

Your marriage has ended and your life must go on. You have a lot of adjusting to do and at times it can seem like a twenty-four-hour-a-day job. Waking up feels different, moving through your day occasionally feels like a free fall, getting through evenings seems like a blur, and spending hours on end (some days) lonely, but always, always different than it had been. You are not alone in this. Your children are going to have their own difficulties getting used to this new "state of affairs." In many ways, however, it is an even more complex journey for them. Depending on their age, they will be hampered by their limited capacity to understand what has happened, why, and what is in store. You will no doubt use all kinds of words to explain what lends itself to explanation, but for the most part they are going to be operating on their "guts"—influenced by the developmental stage they are in. As a parent it is going to be very important that you understand these limitations because it can serve as a helpful guide to your expectations of your children and hopefully broaden your capacity for patience as you learn to tolerate and respect their needs—which will often fall in opposition to your own.

At each stage of development, your child is going to be figuring out and mastering key life skills that will help him deal with his feelings and practical needs. This is his job. But your child will need you to help him do this. No matter what his age, he will need to be fueled by your love. And perhaps most importantly, he needs you to be willing to hear and understand what he is going through.

To understand how your child processes the divorce it is helpful to be aware of the developmental milestones that kids are grappling with at three different stages: ages three to seven, ages eight to twelve, and ages thirteen to eighteen. How he or she is making sense (if at all) of the divorce certainly, at first, will impact most heavily on how your child can cope with your needs. It will also of course help you cope with those of your child.

For example, consider how long a three-year-old can tolerate your being on the telephone versus a ten-year-old. What about a fifteen-year-old? Could you expect your four-year-old to apologize to a friend? How about an eleven-year-old? Now think about your sixteen-year-old. Would getting angry at any of them speed their capacities to truly understand the importance of saying "I'm sorry"? You never let a toddler get near a curb without holding her hand because she has no judgment and poor impulse control. But you can rely on a twelve-year-old's judgment as to when to cross the street. What you know and expect of your child's specific needs and capabilities will inform you about the kind of support and assistance they will need as you begin to build a new personal life.

Emotional Development of Three- to Seven-Year-Olds

By the time a child is three, if things have been secure enough, he will be on the road to "object constancy." You the parent are the love object, the person who has nurtured and been consistent and reliable enough during the ups and downs of life so that your child has learned to hold you inside. When he falls he will have the memory of how you soothed and comforted him. He will know from experiences with you that he is able to get up and brush himself off. This is why nursery school, half day or full day, is a comfortable choice for a prekindergartner. He is emotionally secure in your love and has enough trust in his own skills and those of other adults to be away from you for longer periods. He believes that his world is constant. He will come home and whatever has been promised (preferably you) will be there and he will not be abandoned.

With a divorce suddenly this nascent "object constancy" is threatened. The family is changing. Two parents are no longer occupying the same home at the same time. What was promised (known) cannot be met. For a young child, this is a big shake-up. If you try explaining the situation, you will find that too much (if not all) of the emotional complexity is simply not something a four- to seven-year-old can comprehend. (This lack of understanding could be true for children a few years older as well.)

In addition, there is another major emotional state that rules for the young child—egocentricity. The child believes that the world revolves around him. The sun rises and sets because he's ready to start and then close his day. Everything that happens is in some way connected to his thoughts and actions. Grandma getting sick can be seen as a consequence of something he did. Her illness, he believes, is because he wouldn't get on the phone to say hello last Sunday.

In the case of a divorce, the child thinks, "If I had been good enough to make my parents happy, they would not have separated." A young child will take this on readily, willingly, and inexorably. Knowing that this is what they are grappling with will be invaluable in helping you free them of responsibilities that are absolutely not theirs.

In order not to feel abandoned, your children will need you now, in a consistent and reliable way. Your reassurances that they are not responsible for the changes and unhappiness around them will be critical to their ability to move on . . . and allow you to do the same.

Cognitive and Physical Development of Three- to Seven-Year-Olds

Kids in this age range are moving out into the world. They attend school, play in groups, and socialize on the playground or in a neighboring child's yard or home. They share their rooms and territory with others. They are putting their understanding of language into use. They question things, have specific preferences, and readily agree and disagree with each other. Locomotion is becoming smoother and more coordinated and so they expand their physical world with greater confidence: climbing, dancing, jumping, carrying, and generally arranging external space. Parents, however, are still a primary source of confidence building in terms of how they give support for their child's explorations of the world "out there."

When there is a crisis at home, you will want to keep your child feeling good inside and comfortable outside so that he can continue to seek knowledge of this exciting new world. Your child may regress in behavior and run for shelter to Mommy. He may prefer to stay the baby and remain overly connected in an attempt to make sure that nothing else will change. Don't be alarmed. This does not mean that because there has been a divorce, your child will cling to you forever. It does mean that a big event has affected everyone and that they need care and attention. It means that his vivid imagination and limited processing skills could create emotional gridlock if his worries don't get "played out." After all, we "talk it out." Human beings often feel compelled to verbally go over painful experiences to gain comfort, insight, and freedom from hurt. Because of his less developed verbal skills, a child will seek the same healing through play. Let your child play and don't control the content. There are many ways to do this. You might play dolls using a different one for the mommy, daddy, and child and listen to the script your child creates. If one doll "expresses" fears, ask that doll questions. "When do you have those feeling most?" Your child may feel safer letting the doll talk then revealing the feelings as her own. Give your child plenty of drawing materials and ask her to explain what she's created. If she draws people ask who is sad and who is happy. Ask why. Again, your child will be better able to describe her inner life if she imputes it to things outside of herself. If your child wants to wrestle, do so. She could want to as the direct result of anxiety or a need to be close.

Amy, a four-year-old girl, seemed unfazed by her parent's divorce. She went easily from one home to another for her visits. However, she would become extremely upset if she lost or left a toy or some other personal item behind, fearing that she would never find it again. This behavior revealed her fears. In this case Amy's parents could reflect the emotion that their child is experiencing: "It is scary to lose something important," or "You love your toy and got so worried that he was gone but here he is back loving you again." This allows the child to feel understood, a most precious gift, and therefore have the emotional strength, to process his or her feelings.

Emotional Development of Eight- to Twelve-Year Olds

By this age, your child has mastered many complicated skills. For the most part, they can handle their own hygiene (using the bathroom when the body signals, washing up and dressing themselves, sometimes feeding themselves, at least to a point). They have a sophisticated use of language; they are reading and have for the last few years been interacting with others and honing social behaviors. With these major developmental steps in place, your child is continuing her life with a new focus. She is eager to explore new ways of relating to other children. Sharing obligations through joint projects, creating toys, and playing games together (with new, exciting rules!) feels great. Lemonade stands, neighborhood fairs, or selling cookies to raise money for a bigger cause are all experiences that will help your child build a healthy sense of self. He needs a reservoir of true self-esteem that reminds him he is of value, that others will want to hear and receive what he wishes to offer. This confidence will make it possible for him to take initiative, explore his ideas with uninhibited curiosity and wonder, and freely express the feelings that are percolating inside. He needs to feel his ideas are great ones—and that there is no need to stay silent for fear of being laughed at.

Unfortunately, a child who experiences a break in the family, either through death or divorce, may be infused with a sense of mistrust, worry, and doubt about his own power to make good things happen. He may be in danger of entering this new stage of life with a sense of inadequacy and inferiority. He may despair about his perceived lack of abilities, self-judge mercilessly, and hold himself back for fear of failure. After all, he may be thinking, whatever he is made of has not been enough to make Mommy and Daddy keep the family together. While he can see he's not exactly to blame, he may still be plagued with the notion that if he had been "good enough" he'd have been able to wield the power necessary to keep everything intact.

This is not to say that the divorce will cause irreparable harm to your child. But you will want to stay tuned to the way your child is processing the loss. By remaining aware of the way in which he is interpreting events, you will be in a better position to dispel his misplaced sense of power and responsibility. Knowing when to say, "I know you are sad. I'm sorry. This had nothing to do with you. It's all about problems Mom and Dad have had with each other," can be valuable. You may be helping him hold to his developmental track, sparing his energy for the more constructive tasks that lay ahead.

Cognitive and Physical Development of Eight- to Twelve-Year-Olds

School is the place where a child is expected to behave in an organized and disciplined fashion, and to gain a new base of knowledge. Mapmaking, report writing, presentation assembling, and more are all activities to which he is expected to apply himself with diligence and interest. Children at this age can certainly be silly and playful but the emphasis has now shifted toward something more goal oriented. They want to get good at things. Jumping was fun at three and four and five but at later ages the jumping has a larger purpose—to cooperate in a game, or for a gymnastic or skating routine. Children are learning to commit to an extended term of study. They are practicing bringing real tasks to completion. Part of this training comes from the exposure to different adults who are performing in a range of occupations. Elementary school field trips to meet the firemen, policemen, museum workers, and gardeners who share their experience are designed to help broaden horizons, and to inspire children to imagine a place (or places) for themselves in the future. It is critical for children to make these identifications with people who can do purposeful work.

However, it becomes difficult if those with whom children must identify present confusing portraits. Children may begin to draw faulty and sometimes nonsensical connections.

"If Daddy likes the idea of being a chef and Mommy doesn't like Daddy, if I want to be a chef, will Mommy not like me?" Children will absorb direct messages as well as those they observe or overhear (and sometimes misinterpret). Your discussions and arguments or the physical cues you give off with facial expressions and body language comprise all manner of lessons for your child—no matter what your intention. Your child will often observe and conclude on his own, most times too frightened to ascertain whether or not his thoughts are accurate. ("Dad and Mom are fighting over how to pay for my summer camp. Should I be able to get a job so no one has to discuss it anymore?") Tragically, you may be oblivious to the signals you are giving out and the way in which your child is reading them. She too may not have any clarity as to why she feels so frightened or guilty. Staying alert to any behavioral changes in your child (trouble sleeping, loss of appetite, sudden trouble with friendships) is very important. Taking responsibility for all that you might be putting out into the atmosphere is essential to helping your child steer clear of a negative self-image and remain open to finding meaningful identifications.

In short: An elementary-aged child is on a course to learn his likes and dislikes, and to attach to and identify with adults who can guide them to develop their skills and talents. You want your child to feel free to make healthy choices and explore fully. He needs your attention, support, and approval (uncontaminated by your feelings toward your ex) in order to connect in an enthusiastic way to his heartfelt goals.

Emotional Development of Thirteen- to Eighteen-Year-Olds

During adolescence children struggle for a clear sense of identity. Who am I? Where do I belong in this world? They also struggle to understand and handle intense and complex feelings. Technically, adolescence begins at thirteen and runs until age twenty-one. Throughout these years, a child is focused on how his strengths and limitations can be used in practical ways in work, sports, and social relationships. While issues around forming an identity can surface at different points all throughout our lives, a kind of work in progress, in the first phases of adolescence, a stable core is definitely starting to take shape.

At first, the teen years make themselves known loud and clear when physical changes begin taking place. An adolescent's body changes constantly in ways that stir up many positive and negative emotions: pride, embarrassment, impatience, disappointment, and excitement, to name only a few. There are visible, outward signs, such as breasts, height, and hips for girls, and voice cracks, big feet, and height for boys. Almost everyone is plagued by pimples. Girls start menstruating and boys have wet dreams. Hormones surge. Most teens feel exquisitely self-conscious and tuned in to everybody else growing and changing around them. How do they measure up? Are they faster or slower, longer, shorter, wider or smaller? It is a seemingly endless time of seeing themselves reflected in peers, mentors, and parents.

Their perceptions of themselves and the world transform so rapidly that teen judgment can often make as much sense as the Mad Hatter in Alice and Wonderland. Frequently off balance emotionally and thus very demanding, the urgent fears and desires of adolescents can easily overwhelm them as well as their families. Before teens can consolidate their sense of identity, they will pass through a stage in which they are excessively concerned with being judged. They trip on one stair, land clumsily, and are convinced 100 kids saw it and are laughing at them.

This is a teen's perfectly natural (and predictable) attempt to determine who he is, where he stands, whom he cares about, and along the way, carve a place for himself in his ever-changing world. It's little wonder she may often make little sense and seem propelled by emotions larger than her body might seem able to contain. Jane, a fifteen-year-old sits on her bed doing homework, Mom knocks lightly, enters, and is barraged by, "No! I need privacy! Close the door!" Even parents prepared for adolescence can be reduced to tears from the visceral power of their child's anger. Later, when asked why she was so rude, she may say (if she can verbalize it) that she doesn't know, it just came out that way.

During a divorce it is critical that you stay aware of your adolescent "as child." It is all too easy to fall into a pattern of using these budding adults as confidants, creating a situation where there is a role reversal of needs. You may be tempted to be indiscreet about your dates, assuming your teen can handle it—after all she's dating too. You may forget she has no desire to compare her sexuality to yours. You might belittle your ex because you think your teen can understand. The pitfalls of living with a teen during a divorce can be powerful ones. The good news is you can avoid them with a lot of awareness and a little effort. Teens can emerge from their psychic journey happy, whole, empathic, and productive even with the loss of the former family unit.

Intellectual Development of Thirteen- to Eighteen-Year-Olds

Your teen is likely engaged in conflicts with you, as he is making sense of what he is exposed to from different adults who have varied occupations and identities. He is also trying to stay balanced despite the ups and downs of sexual and physical drives. As teens explore and connect with their talents and endowments, they find places to put their abilities in the world: at school, at jobs, at volunteering, and in social relationships. As they take on different roles, teens will find that their confidence inside can find expression outside. Eventually these successes lead to a career choice.

If, however, there is doubt as to where his abilities might lie, and a morass of other feelings are standing in the way of healthy exploration, your adolescent's progress toward finding his true self could be hampered. He may temporarily and with not much forethought latch onto different and not always appropriate figures and imitate or overidentify with his peer groups, heroes, or romantic figures.

During these tumultuous years of self-discovery, teens will often present extreme behaviors in order to mask their fears by drinking, staying out late, obsessing over "love" relationships, with exploding tempers and odd and sometimes frightening choices of friends. Pledges of fidelity to cliques may push anxiety and identity confusion away, because here they have found a place to belong, to find comfort in being the same. Standing out, after all, is the enemy.

So much is going on for teens that can be missed or misunderstood because they appear physically more grown-up and in many ways seem capable of taking care of themselves. If you are preoccupied with a divorce and hearing echoes of your own adolescent self wanting to break free, it is easy to miss how much guidance your adolescent really needs. Teens act with such bravado because they want to seem invulnerable and independent. However a divorce can frighten them as easily as it does a five-year-old. Perhaps more, as they are old enough to think of the repercussions now and in the future. In truth, while filled with contradictory thoughts, they are quite dependent and watch you very carefully. They see you as a role model even as they appear hell-bent on criticizing you. They want to be left alone, but can feel easily hurt if you do. They act as if they don't care what you think, but become enraged (hurt) with too much disapproval.

Your teen may appear to be grown-up and be quite capable but she is still going through enormous internal psychic fluctuations and physical transformations. You have to be there with a sensitive and stable approach even when she insists you bow out. You are still the anchor; you are still the adult.

One phase of development is a building block toward the next. The goal is for a child to be well put together with a stable sense of self and self-esteem. Healthy people know what they are good at and what and where they need supports and can confidently hold on to themselves even when faced with the ups and downs that life throws in their direction. They maintain a center, a balanced feeling about who they are. You as the parent have to recognize your children's needs in order to help build their confidence and keep them growing strong. They'll do this best if fueled by your ever-present interest, understanding, and encouragement.

Kids Respond According to Their Ages

Your children will see this new life based primarily on two things: their development in combination with the levels of intimacy in the parent/child relationship. The ability to be open and revealing while feeling safe is the basis for intimacy. The choices you make about sharing information and emotions with your children need to be age appropriate. A parent is guided by knowing the child, knowing their needs based on their age and what that child can and cannot handle. It is important to tune in to what they do and don't need to know in order to feel secure. And you have to honestly assess your own needs, how to meet them, and whether or not you are looking to your kids to help you do so. Few things are more damaging during a divorce than asking your children to be anything but children.

How Do Children Understand a Parent's Need for a Partner?

It is fair to say that any new element in a child's life can be threatening. Children, despite their attempt to "control" everything, recognize they have far less control than adults. The smaller they are, the less control they have so when someone new enters, they take notice and immediately begin processing (whether you are aware of this or not) what effect this will have on their lives.

You've been going out with Michael for about five weeks. Tonight, he will be picking you up at your house and you are selecting a necklace that complements your blouse. Your four-year-old, Allison, will be going off with her dad; it's Wednesday. Allison tries on your earrings as you try on a string of pearls. With genuine seriousness, she asks if she can come with you and how come you have to go out with someone without taking "me and Daddy?" You've been divorced for over a year, you've certainly explained this enough times. When is she going to get that you have a separate "new" life?

First of all, Allison is in the throes of "the world revolves around me" egocentricity so she personalizes your absence as a loss, and even, at times, as an abandonment. If you love her why would you need to go out with someone else? She cannot think past her own attachment to you. Your needs are a concept that cannot and will not register on her radar screen. As far as she is concerned, her needs are your needs, end of story. Your putting someone else first feels like an injury. This a common emotional state for young children.

What do you do? Explain and reassure her how important she is but Mommy is a grown-up and needs grown-up time. Let her know that you and Dad are friends (even if you are hanging onto this by a thread), that you love her and will be back for Mommy/child time. Right now, she will have Dad/child time. You might let her have a piece of jewelry to keep with her as a way of holding on to you concretely. Little children like transitional objects to remind them of you and to keep them connected when you are physically apart. And let her know when and where you will reconnect. "I'll pick you up at school tomorrow at 2:20; I will see you then."

Your eight-year-old, Elizabeth, gets annoyed when Sarah comes over for dinner because it means that she has lost her playmate for the evening. She doesn't want to share you. She wants to play games and cook dinner with you, *alone*. "Why does Sarah have to come over?" she whines. You come back with a jolly, "But you like Sarah."

This may be so, but Elizabeth knows a partner means she loses her position or has to share it. Either way she's no longer the star of the show. These are sophisticated ideas all stirring at an unconscious level in a young mind and thus getting played out with behavior full of fears and anger. Mysteriously she may spill her milk all over the floor "by accident" or develop a sore throat each time Sarah is over.

You can use your eight-year-old's life experiences to help her cope with your need for companionship. You can help her to understand the importance of companionship with examples from her life, including how she had three girls over, not just one. You might point out sometimes it's fun to have someone your own age around too, all the while underlining that she is the beloved daughter and no one can take her place in your life. For an eight-year-old your partner is the equivalent of a new friend. If she is secure enough, the hurt of sharing you (make sure both of you share and relate to her) will be an event with which your daughter can cope. Remember, one of the skills she needs to master at this age is sharing and cooperation.

You've been hanging out with your eleven-year-old, Arthur, more and more since the separation and divorce two years ago. It's an easy thing to do. You were too wounded and vulnerable to want to get out there and Arthur could be great company. He liked to go camping with you and is a very athletic child. You hiked with him and went on a bike vacation the first year you were single. You hadn't realized how lonely you had been for adult companionship until you met a woman through a workmate. You are happy about this new romance but at the same time notice how irritable and even depressed Arthur seems. What's going on with him?

Arthur filled a void in your life. You focused your attention on him almost like a mate. Maybe you were using him a bit like a good buddy and he felt special, maybe more special than ever. Perhaps he had let a few friendships go in the process. Hanging out with you alone gave him a way to take care of you and reduce his worries about losing you after the divorce. You became the new team. Now, he's feeling he's not enough. If he was enough, you wouldn't have had a need for someone else. He's feeling a vague sense of inadequacy and blames himself for not being the greatest pal ever.

If you have a fourteen-year-old observing you prepare for a date, his reaction will be filtered through the issues he is trying to consolidate and get straight inside. While teens usually view their parents as somewhat alien, and are not apt to draw direct comparisons between themselves and you, your life might echo uncomfortable or frustrating issues they have not yet worked through. He may feel jealous. He likes a girl he hasn't been able to talk to yet. She might envy you. No one has asked her out yet.

You are a mirror for what your teen is contemplating: moving out into the world with a romantic mission in mind. It's an uncomfortable situation because you're not supposed to be doing what they are doing. This does not mean that every teen will react in the same way, but the parallel behaviors could feel weird to them, arousing intense feelings of competition, embarrassment, or a little too much interest. It could make them want to regress to younger behaviors. An older kid can become clingy but most likely will respond with affected annoyance. "I thought you said you'd be here on Wednesday this week" (even though you can't recall saying any such thing). Then again if your teen is enjoying a very lively social life he or she might be relieved you're busy too. Some teens can grow to feel responsible for "baby-sitting" their own parents!

You would do well to acknowledge his irritation: "I hope I didn't make a mistake in our communication. If I did I apologize and I will be here next Wednesday." You might also say that it's weird to be dating after the marriage but you enjoy adult company sometimes just like he enjoys his friends. Acknowledge it must be "weird" for him to see such a change in your behavior (and therefore his life). Also, check your expectations. Your teen doesn't have to like and accept your new life. He may not want to. Some kids express their resistance by developing a dislike for the man, saying he's stiff or dresses weird, or withdraw and avoid a woman who means a lot to you.

How Do Children Understand a Parent Being Affectionate with Someone New?

Witnessing affection between a parent and someone new is a challenge for any child. How much so depends on the age of the child and the amount of emotional stability and attunement in the relationship between parent and child.

Younger children can conclude the giving of your affection to another means there is less for them. They can become jealous and threatened. When her mother's boyfriend arrived at the door, one five-year-old would announce with great authority, "You can't come in!" This attitude of "my parent is mine and you can't have any" is rooted in the fear of being excluded and abandoned.

Remember that because of the divorce children have lost some-one/something already.

A new person would be wise to focus on the child, communicating he is liked and worthy of attention. Like any new friendship, your partner or date has to build trust piece by piece. This happens over time, not in one or two meetings. In time, if inclusion into family life becomes natural, a young child may look forward to a new and loving grown-up around the house. This same five-year-old who wanted to close the door in his mother's boyfriend's face is now enjoying weekend outings with Mom and Charlie.

Of course there are some instances when a new partner can stir up too many pleasurable feelings and dreams in a child. Sally, ten, lost her mother after a two-year illness. Her dad began to date about a year and a half later. Sally couldn't get enough of the new "woman." Whenever her dad and Teresa had a date, Sally wanted to be around too. Sally craved affection from a woman whose presence in her dad's life set off a powerful wish fulfillment fantasy of having a family with two parents again. For Sally, seeing the affection meant all systems were go (which, by the way, put an extra pressure on the adults).

At sixteen, Joshua resented his father dating. He perceived his parent's split to be primarily his dad's responsibility. In fact, Dad started going out with other women within a few weeks of the separation announcement. Every new woman his father went out with infuriated Joshua and he didn't bother to contain his anger and judgment. He sneered, slammed doors, and didn't give his dad's dates the time of day. Somewhere inside, he wanted his parents to reunite. He couldn't reconcile his loyalties to them. Every time he observed affection, he felt as if he was witnessing his father's betrayal of his mother (who hadn't wanted the divorce but was dating nonetheless). Feelings of his own disloyalty permeated his being whenever he saw a kiss or noticed a furtive hug. He even had to fight vague feelings of disloyalty as he embarked on his own romances. Would he be disloyal too?

Affection between a parent and "someone new" takes getting used to for the two adults involved—even though they may crave the warmth. For children, who don't "need" you to share affection with another adult, it can be anything from confusing to infuriating. What, after all, is in it for them, other than what might seem to be a threat of more loss?

Children of all ages see dates as a threat to their security because for some time they've been "it." It will take them a while to realize that being "it" is not the boon it might seem, and that both of you will benefit from the energy of another person helping each of you grow independently while still staying emotionally close. Still, the possibility of another felt loss is ever present. A parent must stay ever vigilant. A new romance is a seductive, wonderful thing . . . but it's not worth the price of a child feeling left behind.

What Can a Parent Share with a Child About a Relationship with Someone New?

For a six-year-old, connections with the opposite sex are friendships. So your new girlfriend Susannah is your friend as far as your child is concerned. You share things with her like books, music, art, and meals just as your son shares with his friends at school. Your child will perceive the relationship you are having from the context of his own life. If he/she has trouble sharing with friends, feels unpopular and insecure, some of those worries will be played out when you bring someone new on the scene. It is important to let your child know where they stand and what to expect. How is this new person going to affect the current state of your home environment? Will you be including your child and how? Tell her what kinds of things this new person enjoys that overlap with their pleasures. "Hey, Susannah has this dog named Maggie who really wants to meet you." These kinds of statements root children in reality and acclimate them to the change brought by a new person. It gives children a sense of control because they know more or less what will be happening to them.

When Dad started dating someone new, Laura, eleven, actually really liked her. Kate was cool. She was a painter who was happy to teach Laura all variety of artistic techniques. When Laura was with her dad, she got to be in Kate's studio painting and sculpting, listening to great music and having fun girl time.

Then, for no apparent reason, Laura started to resist spending time with Kate. Her dad questioned her many times and Laura made up all kinds of excuses that seemed to him as if she was avoiding the real issue: "I'm not as interested in art," "I have too much schoolwork now." Finally Laura became upset and broke down, revealing that her mother didn't like the idea of Laura having so much time with Kate. Laura felt as if she was betraying her mother by building a relationship with "the other woman." Caught between loyalties, she just shut down. In this situation, where someone new is introduced into your child's life, parents need to act in unison. A parent's jealousies and hurts need to be resolved by the parent, the adult, and not visited on the children.

In order to know what to share with your child about someone new, you must know what else your child is hearing and from whom. Children are best served when they can be free to develop a caring for people that is genuine and flows from their need, not yours. When there is a new person in all of your lives, they need to know that they have permission to connect if they feel comfortable doing so.

When Jill fell in love, she really fell. She became so enthralled with Matthew that she snapped back to behaving as she did in her adolescent dreamy days. This would have been acceptable if she had been single but she was raising a fourteen-year-old daughter. Jill began to confide in detail about her relationship to Stacey. She wasn't explicit about sexual matters but said enough and implied enough for Stacey to be overwhelmed. Because this was new for Stacey she shared some information with her mom about the guys she was dating. Stacey thought her mom expected this from her and she had been used to giving Mom what she wanted. After a couple of weeks, Stacey arrived home from band practice around six o'clock to find Mom having drinks with her boyfriend. Jill was dressed in a short, tight skirt and halter top and was "being affectionate" in a way that made Stacey feel ashamed and embarrassed. It was more than she could handle. She excused herself from dinner angrily and slammed the door to her room; she simply wanted no part of it.

Jill moved so quickly and so openly that Stacey had no time to adjust to the new person. To make matters worse, her mother was applying pressure for her to understand, and observe her mother's social (sexual) needs too. The experience was imposed on Stacey's life in every way. In this situation, Jill was listening only to her own needs and acting impulsively. Teens are struggling with their own impulses (including sexual ones) so seeing Mom out of control is disturbing and frightening. It's too much information, too much exposure, and too far away from the adult/parent role for a child to feel safe.

Do Children See Parallels Between Their Own Sexual Urges and Those of Their Parents?

All humans are sexual from the beginning of life. Sexuality encompasses touching such as cuddling, stroking, massaging, and kissing. The skin is our largest sexual organ. Children almost always feel an interest, sometimes a craving for the warmth of physical closeness to give them a palpable sense of security. They do however, feel anxious and uncomfortable when confronted with their parent's sexuality. Upon hearing from a schoolmate how babies are made, one seven-year-old boy (with two siblings) woke up his father one morning demanding, "You did that to Mommy? Three times?" Children of all ages tend to respond with some significant feeling to the realization that Dad or Mom is intimate with another woman or man.

If you start seeing someone seriously (he's staying over when the kids are in the home) and your children ages three and six are suddenly needing you in the middle of the night to get them water and to comfort them from nightmares, chances are they are aware that someone is in your bed. A child may go so far as to try to get into bed with you and the new partner. Do they realize that they are insinuating themselves into your physical relationship? Not in the way that adults understand it but on some level, they know something is going on that they want to be part of (or not left out of it). They might even want to put an end to it.

Do not invite your children into bed. Maintain a healthy boundary with the privileges of adult privacy. Doors are made and closed for reasons that reinforce the line between people including parent and child. If your child needs comfort, provide the nurturing in their room where you can better preserve the safe emotional feeling. Climbing into your bed usually indicates the presence of fears. A child's own bed offers his best chance to feel secure. He simply may need you to stay awhile and soothe his unspoken and perhaps not understood anxieties.

An older child may also resent this new partner's role, but in a slightly different way—depending on the amount of physical closeness a parent has allowed since the divorce. Jim's wife passed away and left him alone with his nine-year-old daughter, Cathy. He was distraught and overwhelmed. Cathy was having nightmares and she would often come into his bed in the middle of the night. Jim's loss was so great and her grief so intense that he allowed it. Jim figured Cathy would outgrow it. He feared pushing her away.

This had been going on for some time when Jim started to date. His relationship grew quite serious, and as a result he would time their nights together to coincide with Cathy's sleepovers so that she was protected from his romantic interests. When Cathy was aware of a new person "in her place," she began to make visits with this new woman very unpleasant. She became demanding and uncooperative. She complained of stomachaches at nighttime. The physical place she had in her father's life—though not sexual—had helped Cathy feel special. Unconsciously she may have been trying to replace her mother. By allowing his daughter to share his bed, Jim had innocently aroused urges in his child that were unspoken and confusing. Her displacement by his adult female companion injured Cathy's sense of being a wonderful companion to her dad. In this situation, Dad's laxness with the boundaries between the roles of father and daughter (a daughter cannot be company in bed) increased Cathy's emotional wounds.

What can a parent do for a grief-stricken child who cannot sleep in her own room after a trauma? A parent can set up a separate bed in his room as a temporary measure. After a while, encourage the child to sleep in her own bed and read or sing her to sleep. Allowing a child into your bed arouses all kinds of fantasies that, while not specifically erotic, can open up confusing desires that young children have no way of understanding. They can feel rejected and even more deprived.

Your fifteen-year-old Tony gets along great with the man you're dating. It's that guy thing that you can't provide: the love of action movies, sports, and cars. You join them for hikes and other kinds of movies and the trio works. You have been self-conscious about sleepovers because of your son, but after a while, the relationship feels like a keeper and you take the next step and bring your boyfriend over for an entire weekend, including the nights. The first Sunday morning, Tony seems unusually quiet. He says he has tons of schoolwork, excuses himself, and goes to work at a friend's house. When you ask him if he's doing okay, his answers are shrugs and "yeah."

You are confused, but the fact is Tony is even more confused and overloaded. Before your boyfriend stayed over you were all friends. Now, your son is being forced to confront the fact that you are sexual. A parent having sex is not something teens like to think about.

Your son's need is to be out of the line of sight of your sexual life. It is important to be conservative and to try to not display too much in front of a child when they just don't have the experience and skill to handle it. Remember they are in the first stages of putting together the values of sexual/gender love and most teens are not so willing to say much about this. Your judgments must be balanced and informed by what your child can tolerate as well as what is appropriate for you. You can't be selfish nor is it wise to be too sacrificing. In this case, stay with your boyfriend predominantly when your son is not around. It is also fine to have your boyfriend over sometimes, but not until you have a good feeling that your son can acclimate to the new situation.

When and How Do You Draw Boundaries Between Your Needs and Your Children's?

Children would like their parents to meet all of their needs, all of the time. Not only is this not possible, it is not good for them. Kids will have their demands, issue their challenges, and express healthy frustrations, which is good, as it will help to motivate them to develop new skills and ultimately grow. Additionally, they have to know where you stand on things and where you lay down the rules. Right from the beginning of their lives, no matter how joyful parenting feels, you also have to preserve fuel just for yourself. From day one your individual life is negotiated with your children's lives.

A young child has a limited capacity to understand the needs of others. They believe their wishes and desires should satisfy you. They believe you will watch a video with them twenty-seven times and enjoy it each time as much as they do. You and your children are separate people. The process of teaching them about separate needs is slow going. When you want to go on a date, a four-year-old will ask if he can come too. No, you will say, this is grown-up time. There's the boundary. You go off and have adult time; your child has child time and then you come back together and find out about each other's day (with you remembering to stay age appropriate in the information you offer). If you are putting your needs first too often, your child will let you know. Tantrums, angry statements in an angry voice, and generally being uncooperative are the tried-and-true clues. One seven-year-old had such a low tolerance for her parents' social lives that when the doorbell rang she would scream, "Great, not again!" and go to her room, slamming the door for all to hear.

Twelve-year-old Dan was a very anxious child. His parents separated when he was about eight and both had jobs with long work hours. Dan was responsible for picking up his nine-year-old sister from the bus stop and getting her to do her homework before his parent came home. Many nights, he would get a call from his mom or dad telling him to pop some food into the microwave because they couldn't get out of work on time. He never knew which night he would have to be in charge. He often didn't know which weekend he and his sister would be with which parent, again because of work schedules.

After the separation, this family was under considerable stress running two households, and it was difficult to make ends meet. Though Dan managed it, he was being asked to be a mini parent. The boundaries were poor because the adults were letting too much of their parenting jobs fall on the kids. They were not deciding between them on responsibility cleanly and clearly and so Dan was never sure how much or how little he was going to be asked to do. He also did not receive enough appreciation for his contributions; the demands were offhand and simply expected without proper regard for where a twelve-year-old is emotionally. It's fine for kids to have jobs and it is common after a separation for a child to be asked to handle more chores. But it is essential that the new expectations are laid out as clearly as possible, that boundaries are adhered to, and that children's limitations are truly respected. It's not a question of what they *could* do in a given situation, but rather whether or not they *should* be asked to do it.

Donna is a particularly sympathetic and empathic girl. At sixteen, she had already witnessed a heavy custody battle and nasty divorce where her parents had been in poor control of their anger. They fought openly, and too often spoke of their rage about one another to Donna. Their needs overrode their parental mandate: to make a child feel protected and secure. After joint custody was established, Donna's mother felt guilty about the levels of anger Donna was forced to witness. She reined herself in and established proper boundaries, making sure not to overwhelm Donna with too much information that was better kept private. Dad, however, began to ask Donna to be his comforter and pacifier. A shy man who had been married for twenty-one years, this new life left him needy. He placed these needs on Donna and created a terrible conflict for her. When her weekend schedule called for her to be at Dad's house, she felt guilty making plans with her friends or going out with guys. She felt obliged to stay home for dinner and keep him company. Donna felt controlled by his emotional needs. Though her mom had grown to form an independent life, two years after the divorce her dad was spilling his needs all over her and crossing the boundary. Instead of Dad learning to take care of his own emotions, he was relying on a sixteen-year-old too heavily, which impeded a natural entrance into her world of peers and intellectual interests.

When a Relationship Is Over and Your Kids Have to Say Good-bye

It is an understatement to say that a parent has to be very mindful of the new adults they introduce into a child's life. Your children have already had to sustain a major loss. This makes attachment less safe for them, and the aftermath of a divorce is best used for healing, not creating more wounds. However, when you bring new people into their lives, there is a balance that needs to be struck between being too overprotective and secretive about all of your involvements and having people floating in and out whenever.

After her separation, Elaine felt desperate. She had a three-year-old and a four-year-old to take care of all day long. She was exhausted and depleted. Who was feeding her needs? When she met Fred and he was happy to be around her family, she couldn't resist spending a great deal of time with him at home in front of the children. This new relationship staved off the full blast of postdivorce grief and anger because Fred became an immediate fill-in. Again, there were four.

Six months later, when the relationship with Fred went belly up, Elaine felt bereft and her kids were angry and confused. "Where's Fred?" they would ask. "Why isn't Fred here?" Luckily, Elaine was able to help them somewhat understand the situation by reminding them about a neighbor who moved away. The children missed him very much, but at least they could make sense of what had happened with an explanation drawn from the context of their own experience.

After Tom's wife passed away, he was left alone with an eight-year-old daughter. He was grief stricken and not interested in dating for almost two years. At some point, at the end of the second year, he accepted a fix up. The woman was great, energetic, smart, and creative. Ten-year-old Pam was very drawn to her and the feeling seemed to be mutual. Pam often asked to have Julie join them. Tom, however, was realizing that he was still too afraid to fall in love again. He began spacing the dates with Julie over longer and longer periods. Julie recognized what was going on and pulled back herself, deciding to let the relationship go.

Tom and Julie both explained to Pam that they were not going to continue to date. Julie let Pam know how great she felt about her and they maintained a friendship by sending cards and making an occasional phone call. It was sad, but the sadness was not denied and Pam had the benefit of being handled with genuine regard.

Paul and Amanda dated for four years after her divorce. Paul didn't have any children and enjoyed her son, John, eleven, and daughter, Joanna, fourteen. Amanda felt so fortunate to have found a man who she loved and who loved her kids. After a year or so, the kids felt as if they, Mom, and Paul were one family and they had a second family with their dad. Amanda had plenty of time as a mother and enough time to be a romantic partner with Paul. After about three years, the relationship, much to Amanda's distress, began to sink. She and Paul held it together for an additional year to try and shield the kids from another "divorce." How in the world would they adjust to this change?

Paul had definitely become a father figure for the children but he was not a biological parent. There were no rules about continuing the relationship and no court agreements for visitation. John was now fifteen and Joanna nineteen and so both Amanda and Paul felt that the kids were old enough to decide what they wanted to do. Paul was a friend and they were at an age where they could act more independently. In this family, Amanda had the most trouble with the children having contact with her ex-boyfriend. She was angry about the breakup but recognized that it would be wrong of her to influence how or whether her children and Paul chose to stay connected.

Parents have to be ever mindful of their children's perspectives on their dating life. You might like to think it's your personal business, but it isn't entirely. Your children have come off of a trauma too and will feel hurt, mixed loyalties, fear, and confusion. Allowing someone into the picture can feel like anything from infuriating to a welcome relief. Your child's age and developmental stage will largely dictate her reaction to the new person in your life. Be sensitive to her ability to handle the new situation. A lot will depend on your child's age and the circumstances of the marital break. Generally speaking, you would be wise to remember:

- You're the one who needs you to date. Not your child. Don't expect unbounded pleasure in your new life no matter what their age.

- Don't plunge in immediately trying to make someone fill a void. He will initially but eventually things will fall apart, and your kids will be left holding the bag . . . again.

- Try as much as possible not to lean on your children for support. Intimacy will naturally surge after a divorce, but if allowed to cross boundaries your child will be set up for a downfall once you find yourself a mate.

You, your children, and your date (or dates) will not "be perfect together." But you can make it work from your child's perspective with love, consistency, attention, and the knowledge of what you can and cannot expect. They want you to be happy . . . as long as they are too!

3

Date After Date After Date: Mommy, Who's Bill? I Mean, Ted? Or Is It Jake?

You are ready to start dating. The initial pain of the divorce has subsided and you feel somewhat excited. And scared.

Everyone is warning you to take it slow; don't rush into anything because you're vulnerable. At the same time they're also telling you to have fun! See who's out there! You'll feel young and sexy again!

You're wondering what planet they live on. The concept of dating again is certainly thrilling. After all those years of a deteriorating, romanceless, often sexless marriage the idea that you could actually share a passionate kiss with someone new is heavenly. But it sounds as if everyone thinks you're sixteen again. As if this is going to be a simple matter of stepping into a time machine.

The reality is you're still, on some level, spinning from the divorce. Also, you bring children with you to the dating game, and an entire lifetime of experience that makes it impossible to ever be that carefree teenager everyone seems to think you can now reclaim.

You are becoming wiser. And you are not alone. In fact you are so not alone that for the most part you can't make a single decision without thinking about your children. And that includes decisions about dating.

This is both the good news and the bad news. It's good because your children need you to make them a priority. It's bad because in many ways a single parent needs to find a way to sometimes give him or herself priority status as well. You need to date for you and there's nothing wrong with that. In fact it's exactly right. But sometimes you may wonder if this is actually true.

Who Are You Dating For?

There are many single parents who believe they are dating not just for themselves but for their children. Don't we owe them a house with two adults? they might think. These parents view every potential date as a potential partner. This is a big mistake as very few of them will be. Postdivorce dating is your time to figure out what is best for you, to become clearer and more specific about what you need from a companion. It's also a time for you to both enjoy and learn from this process of meeting and greeting, free of feeling as if you owe anybody anything and that includes (for the moment) your kids.

Dating (or Not) for the Family

When it comes to this first stage of dating single parents often have a number of fantasies that make having a truly relaxed time difficult. They imagine they've got the entire future of their family resting on their dating shoulders. . . .

- Isn't it good for my children to see me get out there?

- Don't I need to start the ball rolling so that we can be a real family again?

- Won't I be a better parent if I feel emotionally fulfilled?

- If I start to date won't it drive my kids bonkers?! It will be like screaming, *"See! It's over with your dad!"*

The fact is that dating as a single parent can be an adventure, but also hard work. It can be fun, hurtful, confusing, scary, and disheartening. The other fact is that your children do not need you to date. Sure, they may have concerns about that open space in the family, but your dating is not a fixer-upper. Handled with good boundaries and sensitivity, your dating life won't hurt them of course, but every time the doorbell rings do not make the mistake of assuming you're doing your child yet one more good turn. This would put a ridiculous amount of pressure upon you every time you decide you've had enough of the "dating scene" and need to back off.

Being able to back off is critical to the dating experience. Meeting new people can be exhausting and potentially lonely and sometimes you may simply need to hunker down for dinner with a good buddy—in fact, several good buddies over the course of a few weeks sans dates! If you make dating something you owe your children you will not feel free to pull back and take care of yourself.

Isn't It Good for My Children to See Me Get Out There?

It is good for your children to see that you are not sitting in the corner as a result of the divorce. It is absolutely wonderful for them to see that you are looking outward, that you still have faith in the opposite sex, and that life absolutely goes on with a myriad of social possibilities. But the truth is your children can see you do this with friends and feel just as pleased (and less apprehensive). Each time you get together with another family, or invite people over for dinner, or chat on the phone with friends you are allowing your children to see that divorce does not end life and that you are going to continue to move out into the world. It will serve as an inspiration to do the same. Life can still be fun.

Don't I Need to Start the Ball Rolling So We Can Be a Family Again?

You are a family. You're just not the family you used to be. Your children will be in no hurry for you to create a new one. Think about it from their perspective. Even if your spouse is not around much, the idea of some new adult entering the household and being "in charge" would frighten any child. What if they don't like this person? What if he doesn't like them? What if he has too many rules? What if he takes up too much of your time? You may feel the need to re-create the two-adults-plus-children family, but take care to own that wish yourself. Your children may not be happy about the divorce but that does not mean they're looking for substitutes. They love you and it is healthy for them to face facts. They are for now in a one-parent home that *can* work. If you were to act as if it is something to escape, your children will have a much harder time adjusting. If you communicate love and avail-ability and a "We're doing fine!" attitude they will relax into this new life.

Won't I Be a Better Parent if I Feel Emotionally Satisfied?

A happy, satisfied parent is always better for a child than an unhappy, frustrated one. But your children won't care what's making you happy, just as long as you are. It may take quite some time for you to meet the right person. You've probably been told many times that as you move through your social world you are going to have to find emotional satisfaction in other things besides romance. Work, friends, and family are going to be very important to your emotional well-being. If you feel good about yourself and your accomplishments your children will enjoy the kind of aura you put out. They don't need you to be happy because you have a partner. Of course hidden in this question is often the fear that you cannot be happy without a partner. That is another issue that you will have to come to terms with on your own. For most people, it is much nicer to go through life with someone to love and be loved by in return. As stated earlier, friends who say, "Gee. Do you have to have a man to be happy?" are woefully misguided. You may be quite satisfied in the different areas of your life and still need the intimacy that an adult romantic relationship provides. You may very well feel that only a companion will truly give you this emotional fulfillment. That is your right. But it's important to try and create relationships and follow pursuits that can continue to bring you pleasures and keep you buoyant—for you and your children's sake.

Won't My Dating Drive My Kids Bonkers?

There's the easygoing approach to romantic life where your kids take phone calls and say hello to your suitors. Then there's the closed-door approach. Some parents decide that their children should see none of their explorations with the opposite sex. They are afraid that their children haven't had enough time to realize the marriage is really over and that seeing their parent dating will simply bring it home in the most painful of ways. Others insist that any exposure for their kids will lead to attachments and potential loss. Haven't they been through enough?

The truth is there is no right time to drive the point home that a marriage is over. Certainly you won't want to announce it to your kids with a big party two weeks after you and your mate separate, but you can't hope to protect your children from the realization that their parents are not getting back together. This fact is going to hit sometime and chances are it's better soon than later. For years, appearing that you are disinterested in going out may only fuel their fantasies that maybe you and Dad will reunite. You are going to have to tell your children it really is over, but having a man pick you up at your home is no way to announce your emancipation, even if you are afraid of the emotional confrontation. It's far better to sit your kids down and tell them the truth than to show it to them. Giving them a chance to talk is the better option.

The surprise approach is an invitation to depression, confusion, and heartbreak.

A Question of Privacy

"My dad has a new girlfriend every three months. They're nice but I don't want to bother to get to know any of them anymore because they'll just be gone as soon as I start to like them."

You have witnessed newly divorced friends dating with a vengeance or out of a vast, oceanic need. Sometimes they parade their "new friends" in front of their contemporaries as if they're trophies. "Look at me," they seem to be saying. "I can do this! I've still got what it takes." But it's quite another thing when they bring their dates into the home, often inviting them to stay for dinner, as if to say to their children, "You see? We can still *seem* like a family sometimes!"

Unfortunately a parent who acts out of neediness, desperation, or just plain-old experimentation in front of their children by openly dating different people on a regular basis is offering a crash course in impermanence and instability. One thing your child absolutely needs when the family has been turned upside down is a stable new beginning where a new pattern is established. To ask a child of any age to relate to a veritable stranger, even for an evening, is unfair. What if this man is funny and warm and your child takes a shine to him but at the end of the third date you realize you are ill suited for each other. How is your child to feel then?

For children security means that you and the adults in their world are available, reliable, trustworthy, and focused on them.

Children are on the first road trip toward intimate, romantic, mature connections. They are learning and absorbing like sponges and internalizing ways of being and loving. What they see becomes their frame of reference for how grown-ups behave and treat each other. Quick turnover dating is not a stable picture. If asked, there is probably not one parent in a clear state of mind who would be comfortable suggesting to their children that "It's okay for people to be flighty, turning feelings on and off, forever looking for the next better person." Though you may be embarrassed to admit it, this might be exactly where you are. If so, it's normal. But it's not something you will want to communicate to your child.

As a parent you have to ask yourself what is healthy for your children to see.

And the answer, is not much, especially not at the early dating stage.

You have every right to experiment. In fact, you need to do this in order to figure out what is going to work for your next relationship or next (if you want one) marriage. You also may need to live out some fantasies that have long gone unfulfilled. You might not be even slightly interested in getting involved with anyone. A different person every weekend with whom you can enjoy different experiences (picnics in the park, the opera, a comedy club) may be just what you need. You might like a brief, cozy warm relationship (planned obsolescence) with no pressure of any kind. Then again you might want a quick, passionate one. Or still, something else.

The point is if you let all of your dates enter your children's lives, no matter how briefly, your children will only see a different person coming and going and wonder all manner of things. Younger children may think, "Oh, one man or woman is like any other man or woman." Or, "Does Mommy like all men?" Your teen might think, "Maybe I should just go out with different people too. Maybe I shouldn't really pay any attention to any one person. Maybe it's better not to. Mom probably doesn't want to really like anyone and so I won't either." The message they receive is keep your distance from closeness.

Then again, needy children may have a tendency to want to latch onto the new person or people in order to stave off the loss they feel can be immense. This is an unhealthy solution to loss. These "dates" can become the plug in a leaky family boat. A child may begin to convince himself that any person will do and fail to learn the important lesson of picking and choosing one's close friends based on genuine interests and inner comfort and connection. Such an approach to relationships will set him up for a lifetime of hurt.

This is not to say you cannot occasionally have someone pick you up or drop you off or even sit and chat a bit with your children. But it is important to set this up clearly to your children *before* it happens.

"A very nice man named James is coming to pick me up. He's just a friend. He's good company. I'd like you to say hi" would be a perfectly adequate and casual thing to say to your kids. The message is, this is a person I respect and so I'm going to spend a little time with him. Period. A younger child may promptly ask, "Are you going to marry him?" to which of course you can quickly say, "No! We're just getting to know each other. It's nice for me to have new friends." An older child may warily ask, "Do you like this one?" investing the question with all that you fear is behind it. He knows you haven't much liked anyone so far, and may sense that you are growing distressed. If the relationship is very new, and you do rather like him, there's no point lying to your son, but you can certainly answer in a way that protects your privacy and quells his anxieties about what that could mean. ("Uh-oh, I hope he's not some creep who's going to be moving in.") "Actually, I do like him," you might say, "but it's very early. I have no idea what's going to happen or who he really is." This is a nice opportunity to model for your child a little self-protection. Throwing oneself into a relationship too quickly is never a good idea. If you are uncertain as to the path of this relationship it would be smart to at least part of the time meet him out of the home so as not to create unnecessary tension, concern, or fear in your household.

Children are hurt during a divorce. They suffer a loss. You will want to protect them from another loss, no matter how small, because to do otherwise simply isn't fair. This generally amounts to initially keeping your dating life mostly to yourself so that you do not set your children up for any disappointments or confused messages about the way in which you view the men and women in your life or the role they will or will not have in theirs.

He's There, Your Kids Are There. Now What?

Sometimes enjoying activities with your children will broaden your social horizons because it can bring you into contact with other single parents. The busier the environment the greater the possibility of meeting people. Also you can "cruise" more invisibly, you think, if your children are occupied by the crowd.

It's amazing how they usually aren't. Especially not when you need them to be. Especially when they may sense you have an agenda. A little flirtation around a five-year-old may go essentially unnoticed. Too long a conversation with a single father after the third grade class play will not. Your children will sense an undercurrent in the air and start moving closer. They're likely to be curious but not at all sure what they are curious about. Something is telling them to stick around.

You on the other hand might begin to feel terribly embarrassed. Even, oddly, cheap. Your own child is watching you put your sexual self out there. Sure, you're being appropriate. But you're smiling in a certain way and standing at an interesting distance from this man. He's smiling back. There's a sparkle in your eye. And his. Your attention is focused. And so is your child's. What must she be thinking? Certainly not that "Mom's on the make." It wouldn't occur to younger children in those terms. They would be more likely to see you are turning your attention away from them and toward someone new and at worst find this slightly annoying and at best, curious. Older kids, while noting something, will ofttimes fail to register your warm smile as a flirtation because imagining a parent as a sexual being is just too "disgusting" to tolerate.

But still many parents report feeling naked in front of their child. The best advice is to keep your interactions natural and let your angst go. If you are your most charming self you might actually be modeling some very attractive behaviors for your children.

And then there's the phone. "Who's Larry?" your child wants to know after delivering a message that he's called. "Who's Peter?" he may ask the next day when a soon-to-be blind date checks in. What are you to say?

"I'm dating," you can say brightly. "I'm getting to know a few new people. That's all. I enjoy going out with friends. You do too." This isn't stonewalling. This is absolute truth. Your children don't need to know you're hopeful about one but not the other—that you're excited to see one of them for a second time. What they need to hear is that this is a good thing. A nice thing. And nothing that has much to do with them. At least not yet.

If handled with care and a certain vigilance toward protecting your privacy and your child's right to feel secure, an active dating life should end up being frustrating, exciting, upsetting, fulfilling, disappointing, and an inspiring time . . . no matter what the situation!

You, Your Child. . . . and Who Is That?!

It isn't easy meeting a sane (and available) partner. In fact, it's hard to meet people. Period. So what if this means reaching out right in front of your children, because not to do so would constitute a major lost opportunity?

You're at an outdoor school bake sale and the father of your eight-year-old's classmate comes over to admire your cupcakes. "You must have been baking all day," he says to you and your daughter. Your eyes travel down to his hand. No wedding ring.

Anna is proud and says that the lavender-and-pink frosting was her idea. He compliments her choice of colors, causing her to glow with pride, and then turns his attention to you. "Did your husband help?" he asks unabashedly as a direct result, you are quite sure, of your own naked left hand. "Well, no," you smile softly. "I'm on my own right now." You tilt your head to the side and look into his eyes as if to say, "Your move." But Anna clearly thinks it's hers. "Mom!

We have to sell all of these and this girl wants two." She steps between you and this father as if to scold, "This is hardly the place for this kind of thing." You are forced to turn your attention to the potential cupcake purchasers who are now queuing up.

The most important point to keep in mind in a situation like this is that your child at this point in time is your "date." After all, you came to the event with her. When it comes to eight-year-olds it may be hard to know what they can intuit about the moment, other than the simple fact that your attention has been drawn away. She may realize this man is a "guy" and sense you like that, or she may genuinely be concerned about her cash flow and your distraction is a threat.

The second most important point is that being with your daughter does not preclude you finessing the moment, whether or not your child appreciates your "charming" maneuver.

You might turn to this man and say something as simple as, "I'd love to keep talking but my daughter and I have got to sell these delicious cupcakes. Perhaps we can catch up with each other later?" This statement accomplishes two things. One, it tells your daughter she counts and you're not afraid to say so to anyone. Two, it assures this potential date of your interest in him. Indeed before the day is over you can certainly find a moment to excuse yourself away from your daughter's side to find him and see if an invitation or request for a phone number is in the offing.

In the meantime, as you turn back to your sales position you might try saying to your daughter, "I'm glad we're doing so well with our cupcakes. I was just taking a little social break." This will both assure her of your full attention and allow her to feel that you are with her in spirit. She might say, "Okay," and move on. Or she might be a tad more challenging and say, "You like that guy," as if you should know you're not getting away with anything when she's around. If this happens it's best to be gently forthright. "You know, it must be kinda funny for you to see me paying attention to a 'guy' other than Dad. It's going to take some getting used to for both of us."

However, the real resolution to this moment rests in its aftermath. You will want to create an atmosphere of openness in your house so that your children feel free to ask the questions that concern them.

Generally it's a good idea to ascertain a child's mood or thoughts with a simple statement. Remember that classic old story about the child who asked, "Where did I come from," to which her mother replied with an explanation about seeds and eggs getting together, gestation and labor, and then finally the birth by coming out of Mommy's womb. Upon finishing her detailed explanation, her five-year-old looked at her with great confusion and said, "No. I meant was it Texas or Arizona?" So as you begin, assume nothing. Try to sense what your children need and want to know. Don't pile on too much information.

"There certainly were a lot of people I hadn't met before at that bake sale," you might begin. If your child says enthusiastically, "Yeah! We sold so many cupcakes even to people we didn't know!" then chances are she either isn't thinking about the undercurrent of the day or doesn't choose to talk about it right now. If however she says warily, "What do you mean?" then tell her. "Just that I know you saw me talking to Thomas's dad. He's very nice. I thought you might want to ask me about that."

Let your child know you are interested in her feelings and willing to engage in informative conversations. "Secrets" is not a game you want to play.

Then again, what if your "sale-mate" is your teenager and that nice single father approaches. You have a right to expect your son can allow you a little space, though here too you have to communicate he is still important in that tableau. Chat with this nice man for a few minutes as you continue to run the paint-spinning booth alongside your son. Then turn to your teen and say something like, "You can handle this on your own for a bit. I'll be back in a few moments and if you'd like you can then take off to visit with some of your friends." He may look at you cross-eyed but try not to let it bother you. What are you saying here? In a way you are suggesting to your teen that he relate to this situation from the perspective of his own needs. You'd like to talk with your friend just as he might like to talk to his.

Do, however, keep your word and not become engrossed in some conversation that keeps you away too long from your commitment to your child. Your teen can be asked to wait, but not to tolerate being forgotten.

Again, later that evening you might say, "I hope you didn't mind me walking off with Thomas's dad for a moment?" Your teen may shrug indicating any number of things. He did mind, he didn't mind, he's wondering if you're going to date him, personally he thinks the guy is lame, or what's with you and this need to date anyway? If he opts for this noncommittal response you might want to offer up a simple explanation anyway. "He's a nice guy. We may go out sometime."

Why so forthcoming? Owning up to a simple date will keep your child from fantasizing that a justice of the peace is setting up camp outside your front door. It indicates that your social life at this juncture is nothing to fear or hide.

Your teen will correctly conclude that if you can put it out there with ease and good humor, there's no reason why he can't view it that way as well as understand he can always ask about what he needs to know.

Unexpected Three's Company

Every once in a while circumstances will conspire to unexpectedly place you and a relatively new person in your life, for a few hours, in the same space with your child. If it hasn't been a carefully orchestrated event, you probably have to be prepared for anything. . . .

You've just started dating a very nice woman and have been very careful to keep her away from your five-year-old, Tim. You and your ex share joint custody of Tim and usually you do not plan a date with anyone when he is with you. But this is making you feel too closed in and so you ask her out midweek, assuming your mother will be more than happy to baby-sit. Unfortunately you then discover your mother has a mild case of the flu. You can feel the anxiety flooding in as you hang up the phone with Tim sitting only a few feet away busy drawing.

"Honey," you begin. "Grandma can't come tonight, so I guess you'll just go out with my friend and me." You pause. "We'll have a great time."

"What friend?" Tim asks, predictably enough, without picking his head up. Superman's cape is almost entirely red now. "A nice woman," you respond. Tim says nothing. You notice he's suddenly starting to color outside of the lines.

When Laurie arrives you introduce the two and suggest Tim retrieve some of his artwork from his room to show your new friend. He hesitates for a long moment and you are about to repeat yourself when he takes off like a rocket. You quickly take the opportunity to explain to Laurie what's happened and much to your relief she seems fine with it. "No problem," she says. "These things happen." She says this with a kind understanding that concerns you. She doesn't have children.

Tim is back in a flash. He clearly doesn't want to let you out of his sight. He's never been this quick about anything in his life. Laurie "ooos" and "ahhhhs" appropriately and Tim seems pleased but a bit perfunctory as well. "Thanks," he says quietly each time she admires something new. You notice he's not giving her a guided tour of every line. "See, that's his fist," he'll often say, pointing to a jumble of curlicues. "And that's his power belt." Still, you are putting him center stage and while he might be unsure of what's happening, it is the place for him to be.

A half hour later at the restaurant (a child-friendly one with crayons, perfect to explore your date's Crayola techniques) Laurie seems fine. After Tim resists any attempts at conversation she tries to chat about her dog, Lulu (a name that unfortunately proves to capture how the evening will turn out). Tim instead begins directing all of his comments to you. He talks about how far he can throw a baseball, how much he hates Max in his class, and why he thinks his teacher looks like a giraffe. You answer him directly but also attempt to bring Laurie in by saying things like, "tell Laurie the story about when your teacher . . ." But Tim refuses. Suddenly, appetizer cleared away, he announces in a booming voice, *"I want her to go home."*

Rudeness is not something you tolerate. Nor do you particularly like the notion that your young son is about to ruin your personal life. Firmly you tell him that you're going to finish dinner together, but he becomes more insistent.

"No," he says, pushing back his chair.

"Tim, sit down," you reply, allowing some anger to creep into your voice. You steal a glance at Laurie, who is staring down at her hands now neatly folded on the table.

But Tim is out of control. He starts to cry. "Leave me alone," he yelps as he slides from his seat and starts running for the restaurant door. Tim, you realize, is so worked up with unspoken fears that you cannot hope to change the tide. He's really too young to be pressed to stay. He simply can't handle it. Quickly paying, you all leave and though Laurie insists she can take herself home, you refuse to let her do so. You are determined to let Tim know his behavior will not keep you from being less than gentlemanly or polite to a friend. "It's hard for a child to be around a new person, especially a woman I guess," she offers as you open the car door. But she has that glazed, mildly shell-shocked look. You wonder if you'll ever see her again, but decide against checking on that right now. You both smile weakly as Tim continually bangs on the bar of his car seat.

Once home you put Tim in his safe area that the two of you have devised for other times when Tim has spun into a frenzy. His "calm down" area is in the corner of your living room and is encircled by lovable stuffed animals. You've discovered that playing with Tim and his stuffed animals and dolls is a fine way to get him talking about his feelings.

But it's also important to attempt a comfortable direct conversation.

"Tim, you got so upset tonight!" you might begin.

"I didn't like her," Tim says with that five-year-old absoluteness. "I can see that." You pause. "Did she do something you didn't like? That made you feel bad?" This is an important question because it is showing you are very concerned about what happened to him that evening. Not just how he behaved.

"No," Tim says reluctantly.

Playfully, you might pull out one of the bears and, placing it in front of a tiger, say, "Hi. I'm Laurie. Why did you get so mad at me?"

Tim may start to giggle. "Because."

"Because why?" you might have the bear insist.

You could be quite surprised at what comes out. Tim could grab the tiger and roar anything from "I want to be *alone* with Daddy" to "You're a mean person and I hate you!"

No matter what, it's critical that you acknowledge the message and seek a little clarification. Now, you might pick up the "Papa Bear" and say, "Oh, I see. You felt like she was in the way between us," or, "I get it. You think it was mean of her to be there. Just plain awful of her. Is that it?"

At this point you might want to offer your own perspective on what happened. "I think this whole thing was a big surprise for all of us. Grandma suddenly got a little sick and couldn't baby-sit. You didn't expect to be with Laurie and I couldn't figure out what to do. Laurie is actually a nice person but I don't blame you a bit for being angry we were all together. If we ever go out again, the three of us, I think we should all agree to it ahead of time and think of something fun to do. What do you think about that?" Here you are giving Tim control. That's exactly what he felt he had none of all evening.

Tim will likely be quiet, thinking. You may not hear an answer about this for hours or days. But understand the effects of this kind of sharing will help him master his fears. By addressing his unhappiness directly and through play, you are allowing what got locked inside to gently emerge.

Who Are These Kids??

The central issue of the above situation and many others in which you may find yourself embroiled is, what do you do when your kids behave like heathens when your date arrives?

It's extraordinarily common. You think nothing of having a date pick you up at home. Perhaps it's your first or second date. You are expecting a few quick hellos involving your kids (who are with a baby-sitter they adore), a few uneventful kisses good night, and the quiet click of the door behind you. Let the date begin!

Unfortunately, the moment he enters your home your children begin to scream about nothing, jab at each other, grab your skirt with the strength of Hercules, and more or less make you feel as if you'd like to melt into the carpet. But you're not the Wicked Witch of the West, and you can't very well say they belong to your neighbors, so you need another option.

The answer is threefold:

1. Explain to your date, once you manage to escape, that your children are probably just anxious, nervous, or angry about the fact that you are dating. They don't usually act like this. Acknowledge that you should have arranged to meet elsewhere. This will hopefully ease your date's mind considerably. It will also let him know that you have no problem setting your social life apart from your children. You're not trying to put anyone together except possibly you and him.

2. Understand that your children really are anxious, nervous, or angry. This will help curb your irritation. But the next morning you will need to sit them down and explain that you expect them to use good manners. You might want to ask them if they have any idea why they behaved the way they did. They may or may not have a clue. You can volunteer that you know it's weird to watch Mommy go out with another man but it's nothing for them to get so crazy about. It's just a date. It's just a chance for Mom to have fun, just as they do when they visit with a friend. And then you might also

decide to take the bull by the horns and drag him out of the closet! "I'm sure the two of you think of Dad when another man walks in here. I'm so sorry about that. But you know this is what people do when they get divorced. They meet and enjoy new people. I still care about Dad, but this is a time for me to go out."

3. Compile a list of pleasant places to meet. This could be restaurants, small parks, a cozy bar, or even simply in the lobby of a building. Be ready with suggestions so that neither you nor he have to note in any significant way that dating with kids around can be an added complication even from the get go.

The bottom line?

Your children are going through some major adjustments. Don't bank on good behavior no matter how delightful they are. Sometimes life is too confusing to put a best foot forward.

Gotcha! Online

The hunt. It's not something upon which you will want your children to focus. The idea that you're "cruising" will make most kids of almost any age step back. For younger children the thoughts might be, "Aren't I enough?" or "I thought when it was over with Daddy that was it," or simply a perplexed "Why are you doing that?" For older children or young teens there might arrive the uncomfortable feeling that you're hedging in on their behavioral territory. They're supposed to be "checkin' everyone out," not you!

It's not easy to know how to explain certain dating concepts to your kids but there are useful ways to shape ideas and events for them. You can use references from their own world. They enjoy new friends and might share a ball or toy with a child who attracts them on a playground. Adults and children keep their eyes open and make connections in many ways in order to learn, share, and have more fun. Answering your children's questions by drawing on these universal needs and feelings will give kids a point of entrance into your grown-up feelings (the ones that are appropriate to share, of course). They will "get" quite a lot of it. All children know about being included and excluded, desiring connection, fitting in, and being wanted or not in all areas of their lives. The trick to explaining dating concepts to your kids is to do it in a way that makes it clear you are both at very different stages in your life. You may both be dating but you are the adult and so there is no competition here, or grounds for "you did it, so I can to." However, keeping in mind boundaries of privacy, it can be useful to lend your current experience to your kids who are going around the block for the first time or two. Your movement through the dating world can sometimes be a model, and other times simply stimulate conversation. As a result, your children may feel safe enough to openly communicate their problems to you and process what is the same and what is different in your current lives.

It's late at night and you assume your eleven-year-old son and his teenage sister are fast asleep. It's time to log on to your favorite matchmaker site. A minute later you are scanning through a horizontal list of pictures and thumbnail sketches, supposedly selected just for your viewing by the genie behind the service. Somewhere in this vast array of portraits, you hope, is your next great love affair.

You're completely sucked in. Face after face. You drop a note to this one. Then another one. What's the difference? you think. It's like shopping.

"What's that?" you suddenly hear your eleven-year-old ask from perhaps six inches behind you. 'Who are those guys?"

Before you know what you're doing you move your cursor to the exit box, bang your fist on the desk, turn around, and snap, "Can I get no privacy around here? None?"

"S-o-r-r-y!" your child exclaims with a mixture of hurt and resentment. "I just wanted to tell you I couldn't sleep."

You sigh heavily. That's going to make two of you.

Single parents everywhere are getting caught looking around the Internet on the sly. You don't want to go to a bar, dating services don't seem to work, dances are awkward, and setups or blind dates are hard to come by. The problem is the computer is at home and that's not a place where it is easy to keep secrets. Sooner or later someone stumbles on the proverbial batch of faded letters tied up with a velvet lavender ribbon.

Yours happens to be computerized.

The moment of discovery is probably not the right time to discuss what you're up to. It would probably suffice for the evening to lovingly walk your child back to his room and apologize for acting startled and unusually (you hope) bad tempered. Assure him you can discuss it in the morning and that nothing bad happened.

Then go to bed and collect yourself. After all, what did your child see? His mother, safe at home, checking out the pictures and statements of single men. You weren't drooling. You were concentrating. You weren't sending salacious notes. The one your son might have spotted said, "Hi. I think your profile sounds interesting." In other words, get things into perspective and allow yourself to embrace the twenty-first century.

Then, perhaps in the morning or early that evening you can sit your son down and explain what he has seen. Certainly he's been thinking about it. That can be guaranteed.

"Look, I realize you saw something that looked pretty weird," you might begin. "I don't know what you thought but here's what I was doing. I'm interested in meeting some new adults to have adult conversations and friendships with, just like you enjoy meeting new friends at school, the ballpark, and camp. Only of course I'm an adult and I don't go to school or parks or camps. You need pals and so do I. Since I don't have much time, it turns out that there are lots of places online for single people to locate each other and find out if they have things in common. I was on a website where single people can post their picture and description of things they're interested in. It's common for busy adults to strike up 'conversations' online to see if there is anything they can share." You stop there for a second to sidetrack a bit. "Of course, when I get online, I don't give out any information where anyone could find me." You wait to see if that registers and then move on. "If there is a good reason we move to a few telephone calls."

"So when do you meet?" your son asks. "Is he coming here? Does he like baseball? And are there any Frosted Flakes left?"

You are in the clear (so far). At eleven, he is looking for adults to use as role models and with whom to identify. He wonders if a new guy will be a sports fan like he is. His encounter with you and your hunt on the Internet is fading fast from his memory.

This is classic. Children's minds move a mile a minute. He might already imagine you married a year from now with the two of them at the playoffs.

"Absolutely not," you can answer. "If we do meet it will be at a place away from either of our homes where there are lots of other people so that we both feel comfortable. I'm in no rush. I take everything slow." You stay away from emphasizing too much the safety issue because you will not want your child to fear for you.

Your son shrugs. "Have you met guys yet?"

"A few," you might answer. "No one special."

Your son nods. "Cool," he says perfunctorily as he reaches for his sports magazine.

Unfortunately, what you don't realize is that he's already told your teenage daughter who is having a great deal of trouble coping with the fact that her father seems so unhappy being alone and you don't. To her this is the ultimate betrayal. A computer is a better option than Dad?

Being a teen, Ellie has a habit of locking herself into some extreme positions. And that evening she makes no bones about it. "You're pathetic," she snaps when you mention the computer dating episode. "That's just sick. You left Daddy for that?"

You are well aware that if she had caught her father doing the same thing she would never say a word. You also suspect she's not perfectly clear who left who. She just knows you're okay and her father is not, and therefore you are the villain. This "hunt" that has been disclosed is just another pin in the balloon of her reunification hopes. The fact is her two role models for romantic love (which she is just beginning to explore herself) have blown it, and she cannot let go of the anger.

You quietly tell her that rudeness is unacceptable and then in slightly more sophisticated emotional terms than you used with your son, you confide you've been feeling lonely and that you would like to find a man with whom you can have some fun. (Don't be afraid that telling her how you feel puts a burden on her. That would only happen if you burst into tears, wrung your hands, and said, "Help me, help me!" Explain how you are feeling calmly and matter-of-factly and then inform her how convenient a way this is for *adults* to meet.)

If she comes back at you with the argument that you watchdog her chat rooms as if you're an FBI agent you will simply explain that the sites you go to are carefully monitored (which they are but only slightly) and that adults are better able to spot a scam than children.

If she starts to argue simply tell her the Internet rules in your house still apply. Period.

Rejected! And You Want to Be Alone . . . But Aren't

It is very difficult to experience a rejection, no matter how small, under the watchful eyes of your children. But give them a little credit. They know what it's like being "in" and being "out." They also know what it's like to have a play date canceled, or get yelled at by a friend for no apparent reason. It would be too much to expect of yourself to model nothing but bravery, a stiff upper lip, and an onward-and-upward attitude. You wouldn't want your child to handle hurt in this fashion either. Experiencing hurt is part of a recovery process. That's an extremely important lesson you can offer your children. Probably you've gotten into the habit of regularly hiding your vulnerabilities from your children in an effort to assure them that you are strong and can be counted on. But there's nothing wrong with assuring them that you are a person too . . . with many feelings they can understand. The fact is, once they see you have them, they are far less likely to cry out during their own crises, "You just don't understand!"

> **You have candidly told your fifteen-year-old daughter that you are looking forward to the date you are about to go on. It's your third, and you're hoping it will turn out to be something special. It's now late in the afternoon and the two of you are chattering away when suddenly the phone rings. It's him. He's called to cancel, offers the emptiest of excuses, and quickly gets off the phone. No offer to reschedule. No genuine-sounding apology. You hang up feeling as if you've been punched in the stomach. This is the first guy you've even wanted to get to the third date with in a year. "What did I do wrong?" you think to yourself. You ease into a chair. "What happened? Did he decide I'm not so attractive after all?" Tears spring to your eyes and you look up to find your daughter staring at you. "He canceled," she says matter-of-factly.**
>
> **You feel humiliated. Your own daughter seeing her mother . . . dumped.**

First of all, you might want to excuse yourself for a moment, go into the bathroom and splash some cold water on your face. Also breathe deeply. "Just give me a minute," you might say. "When I come out we can make dinner and talk." Yes, you thought this kind of thing ended the first time around—that somehow dating again, everyone knew the *right* way to treat each other.

No such luck.

You'd like to just pour yourself a drink, or go lie down, but the fact is you have a teenager waiting for you who may already have experienced the same thing, or if she hasn't, certainly will. Everyone does. An extremely upset parent is a scary thing.

"You okay?" your worried daughter asks.

Hard as it is the first thing you have to remember are the basic tenets you would present to her if she'd been suddenly rejected. "It happens to everyone," you would say. "It doesn't mean you are unworthy of someone wanting you. There are a gazillion reasons why some people turn away from connections having nothing to do with you. Maybe he's scared, simply not ready for a real relationship. And if it is something about you that doesn't make you wrong, bad, or less attractive. It means he doesn't view you as the right fit for him."

As you busy yourself making dinner, keep these thoughts in mind and try and patiently answer her questions with a positive message she can apply to her own experiences. This includes letting her know you are hurt. That's part of the human condition.

"Did you have any sign he'd cancel?" Jyl asks.

"Not really, the last time I saw him we had so much fun. I think that's why I'm so shocked," you answer honestly. "Maybe he has a problem I just didn't know about."

"Like what?" Jyl answers. "Like problems at work or something?"

"No, I meant problems inside himself. I think if it had been work he'd have said so. I think he might have been running from me and I don't know why. Could be he's scared. Not ready to have a relationship."

"Yeah," your teenager says knowingly. "Deb just got dumped by Paul and no one can figure out why. He was like all over her a week ago. They'd been dating for five months! Suddenly he's gone!"

This is bound to be a very interesting moment for you. Here you are trading similar stories with your child about dating. It might almost make you laugh. She's dating for the first time, and you're dating for the first time with kids. The question is, is this a time to make it clear that your dating life is bound to be different than Jyl's? Is this a time to make the boundaries clear?

Actually, now, it isn't necessary. You're not discussing whether or not you should sleep with this man. You're revealing yourself to have some of the same feelings that she has—that everyone has.

You're also modeling how to think through a rejection.

"Of course, maybe he didn't think we were right for each other," you might add. If you can say this out loud, it will help both you and your daughter see this thought is not an annihilating one.

However, if it's your seven-year-old who witnesses what happened be prepared for an entirely different conversation. Egocentricity is still in session and you might very well hear, "Doesn't he like you?" She is going to see things from a very simple perspective and one which could cut you to the quick. Here you might want to expand her world by answering, "Things aren't always that simple. I don't think Dan canceled just because he doesn't like me."

"Then why isn't he coming over?" might be the response. "Something must have happened. . . ." Your child is in all likelihood expressing her unresolved questions about the divorce. If she had been better would you have stayed married? If you had been better would you all still be a family? Didn't someone do something terribly wrong? This is an excellent time, despite your distress, to talk to your child about the different needs people have of each other and why some relationships cannot work even though no one is at fault.

Hopefully in short order your child will stop seeing every social disappointment through the prism of a divorce. But for now you might want to separate out what you suspect is going on in her head from the letdown with which you are now dealing. Go for experiences to which she can relate.

"Let's see," you say. "You know how some days Sally comes over to play with you but not Kenny? On those days do you still like Kenny?"

"Yes, I still like Kenny."

"So, you can like someone and still not have them come over, right? Even when you like someone at school, you may not like them enough to be your partner on a project, or think they're the best person to have a sleepover? You can see them sometimes but if you play with him or her too often you find yourself feeling angry."

She might shrug.

"Well, that's a little like Daddy and I. We could not get along with each other for very long. But what just happened to me is something else." You might pause here for effect. "You know how you may decide you simply need a rest from one friend. Maybe you're not sure how much you like her. You need to try playing with other people too. Remember when Lucy told you she needed to play with someone else for a change? You weren't sure why but you felt hurt."

Your daughter will likely nod at this at which point you can say that's probably a lot of what happened just now to you.

Finally you might want to also add that we can't all be liked by everyone nor can we like everyone. That's okay. It doesn't mean anything is wrong with any of us or that we did something wrong. However, you might add, it's perfectly okay to feel hurt. That's how people often feel when someone turns away from them.

"The feeling," you might also tell your daughter (and yourself), "will pass."

Not so Fast: Blinded by Desire

The constant refrain in this book has been to put your children first. And you should. But sometimes, maybe just once or twice, maybe more than that, you will slip. The need for intimacy will get the better of you. Lustful thoughts will overpower your maternal or paternal instincts. Suddenly what your child might think or feel somehow fades into the background (or out of the picture) as you seek to build on an attraction.

When this happens you will undoubtedly be told either forthrightly or subtly by your child that you have made a wrong move. The message will be you may have thought the three of you were getting along, but you are wrong. He'll either say it, "Next time count me out," or sabotage the subsequent week by greeting you sullenly at the door, hating his dinner, and slamming the front door (something you hate) every chance he gets.

Then again your child might like the new trio . . . too much.

The best thing you can do is try to face a mistake head-on.

You have just started dating Jessica and she has invited you and your son to her home, which sports a lovely pool in the back. You

leap at the chance. It's going to be a hot day, you say to yourself. It'll be good for Ben. You are thrilled to be in this beautiful setting with a woman to whom you are extremely attracted. Halfway through the afternoon Jessica suggests the two of you take a walk, also extending the offer in a tepid fashion to Ben. He opts to stay at the pool and you can't say you're sorry. Jessica makes you feel like a sweaty-palmed teenager again and it's wonderful.

When you return to the house (an hour later) you swim in the pool under the watchful eye of the real teenager of the day. Once back in the car for the drive home, almost lost in a lovesick reverie you turn to your son and say, "Jessica is nice, isn't she?"

"Don't ever," replies your son stonily, *"take me with you when all you really want is to be with some woman and not with me."*

A day that had seemed so fulfilling and easy for you had clearly been something of a nightmare for Ben. He simply could not handle being exposed to your romantic life. He had felt uncomfortable, left out, and angered. Your mind immediately, for some reason, goes back to the day the official divorce papers arrived two years after the marriage had ended. Somehow those papers in black and white with state seals had hit you in the gut. You grieved for days all over again. You wonder if this date somehow felt the same way for Ben.

You're into other women and Ben had to face that fact all afternoon.

"I don't think you were ready for this. I didn't prepare you," you say simply.

"What? For dating some woman in front of me? No, I guess you didn't. Of course even if you had what was I supposed to do? Watch it like a movie?" comes the piercing and fair response. "Mom would love this," he adds.

There's the other problem. Your son is likely feeling disloyal to his mother. In a way he may feel a party to an act that would have hurt her. Now what does he do? Tell her about it? Keep it to himself?

What he does is up to him. The worst thing you can do is to ask your child to keep a secret from the other parent. Nothing will provoke anger, confusion, and guilt more quickly. But what you can do is be up front about your mistake and center your words on it being *your* problem and not your child's.

"My social life should definitely be something I keep to myself until and unless I am sure there is someone in my life who is going to be very important. It was thoughtless of me to bring you along. You're right to feel put out. The fact is I wanted to spend time with you and Jessica invited us and I like her so I said yes without thinking."

Your son looks at you. "Words. Just words," he says like the sullen teenager he is. But you plow forward.

"As for your mother," you add, "I don't know if she's going out with men at all, but if you feel the need to talk with her about this go ahead."

You might also want to tell your son that you hope in the future that anytime you do something that ticks him off (you will want to avoid words like "hurt" as few teens like to appear so vulnerable) you hope he will tell you.

But now consider another version of this story. You took your eight-year-old daughter, Maria, to Jessica's house and the two of them had sat together giggling and painting fingernails. After lunch you left Maria with Jessica's housekeeper and went off for that romantic walk. When you arrived back Maria seemed fine but on the car ride home in response to you saying, "Jessica is nice, isn't she?" your daughter replied, "Are you going to marry her, Daddy? I like her house. When can we go back?"

For younger children it is important to keep introductions gradual and camouflaged. Children can become enamored with your "friends." It can happen very quickly. Even if a woman or man is presented as a friend, if your child takes a shine to this person and if your romance doesn't gel, it's another loss for your child. You will need to think carefully about whether you want to present your children with a series of these kinds of events given the loss they have already suffered.

In a situation like this, rather than concentrate on self-blame, you will want to gently repaint the scene your daughter has in her mind.

"Honey, Jessica and I are just friends. I think we'll probably see each other again now and then but I'm certainly not thinking about getting married! I'm glad you like her though. I think she likes you too. Maybe next week you can paint your nails with Aunt Lilly. She's coming for a visit, you know."

It would be good if you could underline the fact that there are other women in your life with whom your daughter can enjoy certain activities.

As a parent you are always a tuning fork, but in transition times the sensitivity meter has to be turned up high. It's inevitable that kids will have more feelings as they have more exposure and interaction with your new love interests. During the Date After Date After Date stage, however, it's best to keep those contacts to a minimum.

4

A Little Romance:
He's Here for Dinner Again?

I^T's hard to believe, but suddenly you are back in the world of
relationships. After your breakup, life with the opposite sex
had begun slowly. It started through introductions and the casual
meetings that take place at work, the supermarket, the gym, and
at the kids' school benefit sales. You dated everyone (it seemed)
from your friend's second cousin to the owner of your favorite
bistro to the alarm repair man. You experienced many "one time
and then never again" dates, "maybe, I'll try again" second dates,
and the "time to make a decision" third dates and concluded that
most were not for you. Those with a tiny bit of possibility became
minor involvements—for practice, you told yourself. But now,
you have found someone with whom it is worth spending more
time. He was introduced to you four months ago at work by a
friend who was "watching out for you."

You're thrilled, and chances are you are leaning toward one of
two approaches.

That "He's the One" Feeling

You may very well have all the symptoms of "this may be the one": heart palpitations, happiness, fear, and the feeling that you're about to step into a lovely, scary place. You can't know what is ahead of you and certainly feel you have had enough hurt, but you know you can't hide forever. Still, you wish it were safer. Can't everything be "known?" you ask yourself over and over beseechingly as if you can actually bring this about. Will this new relationship you've found be a lasting one or at least a constructive learning experience and if not for all time, for some significant time? You hope you won't get scalded. You are too jaded to believe in "happily ever after" but you've been so lonely and so in need of a wonderful companion that it's hard to contain your adolescent instincts. Those teenage years you thought you couldn't recapture? Well, "they're back!" And their name is Bill. You feel both lighthearted and on the edge of a precipice. You know you are throwing yourself into this involvement and realize it may not be wise. But you welcome the rush. Life has felt so emotionally and physically barren on so many occasions. The uncertainty of what will happen may at times seem intolerable, but holding back would be worse. You take a deep breath and square your shoulders. Ultimately, you're an adult . . . not a teenager. You can take care of yourself.

Then you remember the kids.

It's one thing for you to take this romantic ride but how do you explain the possible impermanence to your children? They will see you're with Bill to the exclusion of anyone else. Picking up on your cloud-nine countenance, they will want to know, "Are you in love?" Your younger child may ask, "Will he be our father?" with just a Mack truckload of concern. "Is he moving in?" your older one could ask with dread seeping from his every pore. The truth is you'd like to keep your boyfriend tucked away but because you think he may actually be "the one," you want to have him around all parts of your life to assess the fit. The problem is, will your children be able to view this new person in their life as a "constructive learning experience" if and when at some point he moves out of your life? Then again, do you have to think about this when this wonderful man just might be in your lives for the long haul? You can feel this possibility in your bones . . . you think.

Or maybe it's just that you're ready . . . and any decent port in the storm?

That "Well, Okay! The First of Many!" Feeling

Karl is turning out to be the most interesting person you have met so far. You are tremendously compatible with each other and while he may not be a keeper (he seems a confirmed bachelor) he is a kind and steadfast companion. That's all you really want right now; someone reasonable and entertaining with some major physical chemistry. "Happily ever after" isn't a banner you believe in waving these days. Yes, sure, you hear that everyone wants true love and romance; it's very popular. But after all the complexities of figuring out your needs, your ex's needs, your children's needs, it all seems too complicated and exhausting. Right now, some fun is in order. It feels exciting and that's great. Finally, here is a person who has some of the basic virtues that you have been trying to find in a companion. Karl is appealing; he is smart, does fascinating work (which he actually chose and likes), is physically attractive and so far reliable and trustworthy. He says he will do something and he does it. "I'd like to get us tickets for the art show at the museum for Friday." You offer full approval, "I'd love that." By Wednesday, he confirms the plans. He wants to show you a good time and he's succeeding. You think, this is what people must mean when they talk about a flow. A relationship just moves forward with grace and ease. You like it. Being exclusive with him is a joy. But are you really exclusive?

It's time to think of the kids. How long can you and should you keep this man under wraps? He calls, they know his name. He picks you up, and they look out the window. "Why do you see him so much?" they want to know. "Is he your boyfriend? What's going on?" This gives you pause. What *is* going on? You're involved in a relationship that has intensity and intimacy but probably won't be the one for the long haul. Still Karl holds an important place in your life. How do you (or must you?) introduce him into your life with your kids?

Telling It Like It Is
(But What Is It Exactly?)

It's good for your children to see that you have survived the divorce with a positive outlook and are back out in the world with friends and "friends." It is another thing entirely when that "friend" regularly enters their lives in a more intimate way. They didn't select this person, after all. Why wouldn't they think, "Who is he really and what is he doing hanging around?" A child has all kinds of instincts and needs that will get stirred up around a new person. Sometimes the reason will be the need to fill a void and have another grown-up around to bring some fresh air into the sometimes close atmosphere of single parenting. Other times it will be the fear that they will no longer be of primary importance to you. They may experience resentment and uncertainty that as your life moves on, so will it affect theirs. A little diversion can be refreshing and a child might genuinely enjoy relating to a new person, or it can suddenly give birth to anxieties and unhappiness.

Children are very vulnerable and can easily personalize losses. Whether they like him or don't, can accept him or not, how do you explain a person coming into your life and theirs who you really enjoy and like but who might inevitably move on? How do you help them roll with the emotional punches of *your* relationship life? Especially this first one. Before we go any further it is important for you to consider this warning:

CAUTION:
First Relationships Postdivorce Are Often
Not What They Seem

This is not to say this person won't be "the one." But if he is, it will be because of a near miraculous confluence of elements that don't usually occur first time around. People after a divorce are too raw and needy in ways they are barely aware. They are often too scared, confused, naive, conflicted, and inexperienced to make even a great match work. We all know it takes more than the "right" person to make a meaningful relationship happen. You are dealing with so many complex issues after the loss of your partnership: time, trust, betrayal, dependency fears, inordinate dependency needs, defiant independence, just to name a few. The fact that you can make that first relationship be a good one should be considered a major success no matter what else happens! So keep this in mind when interacting with your children. They need you to be grounded—and while you are entitled to dream, try to remember that to include them in the fantasy might not be fair. For them it's all too real.

Despite the above warning, however, you should and can find a way to explain the presence of this person in your life that speaks to your boyfriend's importance but not necessarily his permanence. If you were to say nothing you would be hiding feelings and keeping secrets, which leaves too much to the child's imagination. He or she has a limited frame of reference (maybe he has one friend whose mom has a boyfriend?) and as a result things can become disturbingly uncertain. Why isn't Mom talking about this man? Is he bad? Is what she is doing bad? Does she want to leave me out? Will he like me? What if he doesn't? Am I going to be less important? Am I supposed to pretend I don't notice? Is it bad if I ask questions? What if she gets mad at me for asking?

Your children should not be left to wrestle with these and many other questions, all of which they will be unable to answer. These questions can fester, giving way to feelings of fear, anxiety, sadness, anger, insecurity, and worthlessness.

So, the question at hand is how *do* you explain your romantic partner's place in your life. You have been seeing this significant other for three months and your children, you can tell, are now wondering what's going on. No one else has shown up for weeks. "Toto, I have a feeling we're not in Kansas anymore" is the spirit permeating the house. What now?

For one thing, don't start the conversation five minutes before your boyfriend's next arrival. As awkward as it may be for you to field questions, it's important to let the kids say what's on their minds. Remember, you don't have to explain your intimate feelings in graphic detail. They simply need an opportunity to say what's on their minds and you, as the adult, will have a chance to put forth a picture they can both understand and feel free to question. They need you to "frame" the situation and put what's happening in some perspective.

One weekend morning your fourteen-year-old, Adam, ten-year-old, Jenny, and eight-year-old, Joshua, are having breakfast together. "Tomorrow, Sam is coming over to join us at the lake," you say. "You know that he is a good friend of mine and when I go out for an adult evening, he is the person I have been spending quite a lot of time with."

"Yeah, he's your boyfriend," eight-year-old Joshua offers casually. He says this in such a world-weary way, as if he's made the remark a thousand times before. This is a tip-off that your boyfriend is a pretty big deal.

"I guess you could say that but I want to let you know that he may not always be my boyfriend. He's more of a close friend who is a man and since you have answered the phone when he calls and you know about him, I wanted you to get a chance to meet him. He's fun to hang around with and he likes kids but that doesn't mean I will be with him permanently. I just don't know that yet." You will be in awkward territory here because children often see things in black and white terms. For them and for most of us, getting a handle on the subtle nuances of relationships can be confusing. Even for an adult the difference between deep attachment and appreciation versus real love is often elusive. How many times over the years have you spoken with a friend who is puzzled about why they don't have the right feeling for a woman or man in their lives? "She's kind, smart, a good lover but there's just something that isn't quite right, that tells me I can't go ahead." What is that missing piece? Is it your fear or that chemistry/soul connection that has been written about and pondered over since the beginning of time? It's a complicated business and one that requires real romantic experience to wrap your brain around its nebulous borders. So here you are in the kitchen with your perplexed kids who are genuinely trying to "get it."

"If you go out with him and like him and he's fun to hang around with, why wouldn't he be permanent?" Jenny asks.

Your fourteen-year-old is acting like he couldn't care less but doesn't leave the room. There's something about this discussion that is holding him here. He has an interest in girls but an icky feeling about the idea that you date too. Your romantic life is likely going to catch his attention and repulse him at the same time in a mind-boggling if not mind-blowing way.

You continue, "Think about the friends you have. Have you always liked each of them the same amount?" "No, Lisa is my best friend now," Jenny quickly pipes up, "but last year I liked Alice better."

"Really? Why the change?" you ask. Here you are getting your children to think about and understand what makes connections change, grow, or sometimes fall away. You know for a fact that your daughter enjoys Alice and certainly includes her and considers her a friend but the bond with Lisa is just stronger; it's just the way it goes. Jenny looks pensive.

"I get the feeling you discovered you and Lisa can get on each other's wavelength like perfect musical notes. I think you discovered sometimes you and Alice have too many differences." Jenny nods in agreement with this concept; she gets it.

"I have always thought Pete is the best," your son Joshua pipes up, almost challengingly. It's as if he's saying, "You may not stick with people but I do." You know he misses his father.

"Sometimes you meet a person who is right for you, period. They can accept the way you are and allow for you to change and grow and vice versa. You can do the same for him or her. That's very special." You pause. "I hope to find that person." You look at your son. "For a while I thought Daddy and I would be like that but it didn't turn out that way. We went a real distance together and that allowed me to have the joy of each one of you, so that's a great thing." You say this because you know it's best to acknowledge the elephant in the room.

"Could you and Sam stay together?" Jenny asks.

"Well," you continue, "I'm still exploring how much Sam and I have in common but I do like him and that is nice for me," you say. "We may get closer or decide we're not the right match. We don't know yet."

This is a good start to bringing a more significant person into the picture. You have guided your children into a sophisticated concept about human relations that will give them the freedom to trust their instincts about what they like and need from people. Too many people allow themselves to become trapped in relationships that bring them little happiness. Not every nice person, with whom you can enjoy yourself, is a person with whom you need to stay. The door is open for them and for you to make choices based on authentic feelings

In a day or two your companion will appear and your children will wonder how deep the bond will run. This is good. You don't want them to become attached to a fantasy. But they will also have another concern. What does a new person for you mean to their lives? They are kids and the world revolves around them. Your job is to gently help them make room for others who matter, and still hang on to their own sense of importance in your world.

The Family Outing Plus One

For some time now it's just been you and your children stepping back out into the world. But now there's a new person coming along.

During your first time out, it would be a wise choice to focus on the kids. It would also be smart to share this plan with your companion so that he is not put off or confused by your behavior. You would do well to plan an activity that can be shared and enjoyed together. Conversation will hopefully arise naturally, springing from the shared experience, and will give your children and your guy a chance to get a feel for each other. If things go well you can gradually move from the more casual outing to include your friend in slightly more formal times. He might join you for dinner, or come hang out on a Sunday afternoon. However, take care not to invite him over all the time but rather, here and there. Keep some times separate and devoted to you and your children. If you move slowly, your kids will be more likely to acclimate themselves to the new person in their lives. In the best of all worlds, your child and this new person may find something special to share with one another: gardening, playing the piano, or the love of movies. Such commonalities begin to build the foundation for most of the relationships we enjoy in our lives. A genuine but moderated relationship between you and your new companion and your children can be a very nice thing (though of course you need to be careful that your children don't become so enmeshed in a fantasy of forevermore that a split could seriously hurt them).

Of course sometimes good feelings simply don't happen. There is continuing tension and no one, perhaps most of all you, is enjoying the time spent together. This is quite common and will require a different approach.

There's Trouble in River City

Problems between your boyfriend and child can easily exist. It may not simply be that your child doesn't happen to like him. It's may be that she doesn't *want* to like him. Combine this with a boyfriend who may not be skilled with children and things can get pretty dicey. You are probably going to want to wait a while to see if the tension subsides. If it doesn't, the best course of action is to step in, talk about what you see, and come up with some solutions everyone can embrace. The one thing you cannot do is keep waiting and waiting for your child's disdain to evaporate. First of all she might think you don't notice, or that you do notice and don't care. Second of all she may be trying to tell you something, and by ignoring her behavior you will be shoving aside her thoughts and feelings.

Joanna had shuttled back and forth pretty comfortably between your and her father's homes since she was five years old. Now at twelve and on the brink of real adolescence, she is beginning to push away from you. Part of her need for emotional separation was being acted out through the heightened tension between her and your dating companion of the last five months. There had always been an underlying wariness on Joanna's part about Matt: a combination of fear, confusion, and guilt (for being disloyal to her dad). Sometimes, it went underground and you breathed a sigh of relief, believing it was gone. Then disappointingly it would reappear. But now, it's out in the open. Joanna is literally sticking her tongue out at Matt in public places whenever he says something that annoys her. Matt, furious and feeling helpless, uses sharp words or muted anger toward Joanna. He's getting very short with you as well. However, there are many times that Joanna and Matt actually have fun together.

The only thing you can do is bring the problem out into the spotlight. Your daughter is acting like a brat, and your boyfriend is hurt, resentful, and you're afraid, perilously close to a "Who needs this" attitude. It's definitely time for a heart-to-heart with everyone.

First you take on your daughter. You do so directly, but being careful not to place the blame at her feet. "Look, you are my daughter and are the most special person to me. No one can replace you and I love you. But Matt is very special to me as a friend and confidant, and more and the tension between you is getting really bad. What do you think we all should do here? If I'm contributing to the problem I want to know how and what I can do." You can sit quietly and discuss such things as how much time to spend together, what bothers her about the way the two of you act, how she feels when she hears whispered terms of endearment. Hopefully you can reach some middle ground. For instance, no holding hands *everywhere* you go together and perhaps keeping the get-togethers to a minimum.

Later, you speak to Matt about how infuriating it must be to have this child treating him so disrespectfully and angrily. You try and explain her conflicts and ask him to try and not fall for the bait. Hopefully he will acknowledge that snapping made him feel lousy anyway and that it is he, as the adult, who has to try to maintain some cool. Of course he may also be slightly scared off by the level of unpleasantness he is experiencing when he is with the two of you. Either he'll stick it out or he won't. Obviously you can't make a person do something they don't want to do.

The bottom line is that you cannot continue sweeping tension under the rug (the pile will get so high, you'll just trip over it anyway). Acknowledge that it is hard to mesh sometimes and that we all get out of sync. You cannot force Joanna to like your companions. You can, however, expect her to be polite to your friends and at the same time help her shed light on what's bugging her. It's the only way to deal with the problems . . . and add safeguards to your relationship!

Sleepovers?

If holding hands in public is a problem, your date staying over can be a tsunami. Having someone spend the night signals something major for children. Depending on their age they may not know exactly what, but they will know it's an event worth noting in a big way. At the most basic level, you are having someone in the place that was formerly occupied by the other parent. All sorts of unconscious anxieties and comparisons will begin click-click-

clicking away in your child's mind. Issues of betrayal, disloyalty, and yearnings for the "real" parent will to a greater or lesser degree be drawn to the surface. It's tricky territory for a child to witness (or imagine) intimacy in the same geographical location he had seen his parents: in the same bed.

If you want to set the stage to bring about the most promising outcome, it's best to do so gradually. Your partner should first hang out late a few evenings, then help to tuck young ones into bed, and then finally, if you're sure this relationship has some lasting power, spend the night. This approach can eliminate a lot of confusion—though certainly at no time will the first sleepover feel "natural" to your children and it matters little whether it comes early or late in the relationship.

However, if you make a decision to go ahead with a "sleepover" early in your relationship, how do you inform your child that you will be having an overnight guest? You may not always have to make it clear. If you have a young child at home, who sleeps through the night, and a boyfriend who's willing to leave before *Rugrats* is on, he can probably spend the night without anyone being the wiser.

If you don't feel inclined to take the chance, for a very young child, you might simply say, "Jay is staying over tonight as my guest." Then follow her lead and see what she asks, says, or does. Don't be surprised if you get summoned in the middle of the night to fetch water (several times). You may have an additional little person coming to visit as in "things that go bump in the night." Again, this is not a neutral event and your child will be curious or even threatened by this other person who is so obviously close to you in all ways. Your child may want to join in and not be left out. She may also feel quite rejected when led back to bed.

An older child will know what's going on and, depending on age and developmental issues, will experience different degrees of discomfort and embarrassment. A ten-year-old boy may shrug his shoulders and hope that Andre will shoot some baskets with him in the morning. Certainly he'll know something different is happening but he may not consciously connect with it in any major way. An adolescent on the other hand may say, "That guy is staying here?" This might be followed by an eye roll and a sigh, signaling major disapproval. A teenager's own sexual feelings around romantic love are pretty high-pitched. One mom informed her thirteen-year-old daughter that Matt would likely be spending the night on Friday. Her daughter looked at her with disdain and blurted out, "Don't even think about it." The whole idea that her mother could be sexual right before her eyes was unbearable. You will want to ask yourself how comfortable you really are going back to your bedroom for a night of passion with your teenager a wall or two away. These are all-important factors to consider before having a relative stranger (in the eyes of your children) for an overnight.

Just imagine the morning and everyone attempting to chat over the Cheerios. Are you up for that?

Of course you don't want to give your children unnecessary power and control over what goes on in the house. But having a daughter who is embarrassed and edgy, refusing to stay at the kitchen table after abruptly pouring cereal and angrily marching away isn't fun. As one mother put it, "Even given the passion that night, the awkwardness in the morning just wasn't worth it."

It is not realistic to believe that children will remain neutral when you have a boyfriend sleep over. It's not without its complexities for you either. If you draw on your own experience in relationships, pre– and post–physical intimacy, you will usually find that you are more vulnerable and have rising emotional stakes once you have had a sexual encounter. It's human and primal for something to shift when physical intimacy enters the picture.

Adding your child's deep confusion and fears into the mix might create a situation you don't want to handle. Here are a few things to consider when deciding whether or not to have your companion spend the night.

Do you want to and are you ready to take on more emotional challenges around parenting?

Do you want your children focusing on your sex life? Are you prepared to frame and explain and work with their vulnerabilities as well as your own?

Do you want a person who may not be permanent to enter your children's lives with the illusion that they will be around and hold a special place?

Do you want your teenager to watch you switch sexual partners?

It isn't easy to stop and think of the children when your own hormones are surging and your need for physical closeness is intense. But you will want to consider all the possible ramifications before you act. That way you'll be ready to address your children's concerns before they overwhelm them and you (not to mention your friend).

There *are* ways to get through the touchiest of realizations ("He slept here?") to the most annoying (your teen treats your lover like dirt) to, for some, the most emotionallly confusing (your child's been hiding your ex has a new love.)

The name of the game is Secrets Are Dangerous, But Too Much Truth Is A Burden. Your job is to find the middle ground.

Caught in the Act

"Careful the things you say, children will listen, careful the things you do, children will listen and learn." So writes Stephen Sondheim in *Into the Woods*. It has been our experience that kids (until it becomes too painful and they block it out) "know" a lot more about what's going on beneath the surface than we think. They can sense emotions and atmospheric changes in the house. They do not always fully know what is happening but they pick up on shifts in feeling, tone, and behavior. Assume if you are within earshot or anywhere in their line of sight, they will hear and see. There is no point in pretending otherwise unless you want to model a sneaky and indirect way of handling complicated events and emotions. Of course you could leave it to your children to figure out what's happening, but what are the chances that they will process what they see or hear correctly and thus stay on a healthy course free of rancor toward you?

This is not to say you have to make public announcements about everything you do, or not try and keep a few things private. Sometimes you should. It might even work! But anything that happens in the home is hard to hide. Things are in the air . . . everyone breathes them in. So, if you're caught, or even think you're caught, take a deep breath and face it . . . delicately, carefully, and in a way that tells your child what he needs to know . . . and of course, no more.

Where Did He Sleep Last Night?

You had intended for your lover, Ted, to leave before your eight-year-old-son, Ben, woke up. Unfortunately, time slipped away, and though Ted is indeed on his way out the door very early, Ben has chosen this morning to greet the dawn. He takes one look at Ted and says, "What are you doing here?" Ben appears, you think, confused. Maybe even upset.

Or maybe he isn't either of these things. Maybe it's you who are confused and a little upset. You had intended for your lover to escape unnoticed. You'd spent a lovely night together, one in which you had done your best to block out the possibility that your child could knock on your door at any moment. He didn't, and you were pleased. But now, here he is in another unexpected way and you are not prepared. Or are you? This does not have to spell disaster, or even a problem. The first order of business is to answer the question with as little information as possible so that you can judge what your child really does and doesn't want to know.

"He's just leaving" would be fine.

"Did he sleep here?" your son asks.

"Yes. It got too late for him to go home," you say simply. "He slept on the couch."

"Oh," your son answers with satisfaction, more or less.

You decide not to offer anything more unless he presses. He doesn't. You move right on. "What would you like for breakfast?"

However, what if your child studies the couch and frowns, asking, "But where are the pillows and blanket?"

"We put them away." And that should be that.

Where your lover slept last night is really none of your child's business. He might like to bring it into focus, but that doesn't mean he should be allowed to do so. This sort of fib should not compromise his trust in you. There is nothing to be gained from him knowing graphic truths and much to be gained from making it clear there are facets of your life in which he does not belong. He can express his concerns or worries without being informed of the intimate details of your relationships.

He has seen nothing but your lover getting ready to leave and while, especially if he is a little older, he may suspect the two of you slept together, there is no need to confirm this, unless you choose to.

And why would you do that? Perhaps your son is fourteen-years-old and looking at you, clearly skeptical. He knows the truth, though perhaps not quite how he feels about it, and he just wants to hear you say it. He's been waiting to face this confusing moment for a long time, and he'd like to get it over with. Mom does have a sex life. Imagine that. She is going to sleep with someone other than Dad. Or maybe he just wants to know, so he can judge where you're at with this relationship.

"Yes, he slept in my room," you can say. And that is all you say. If your son wants to speak with you about it, be open, but keep the topic to feelings, not sex.

"I like Ted very much" is appropriate.

"Adults like to have sex too" is not.

"It's nice having Ted's company," communicates the tie between emotional and physical intimacy. It underlines your desire for companionship.

Your son is at a vulnerable time in his life when he is trying to make sense of his own sexual impulses. As much as possible you want to draw attention to the critical relationship between feelings and physical closeness. You also have to make it clear that the two of you are at separate stages in your life, that you approach physical closeness with different degrees of experience and understanding and that he cannot necessarily do as you do.

"I recognize that we are both trying to have a social life, but you have to see the difference between us. I am a grown woman with lots of experience. You are starting out and though you are a terrific and smart kid, there is a lot to learn. The way I behave is based on my being an adult who has had involved emotional relationships and as a teen you will explore and find your own way and what's best for you with my help and support, when you need it."

Let Me Out of Here!

"I wouldn't give up my children for the world."

How often have you said that to your friends or relatives after bemoaning your loneliness, or the fact that you have too much responsibility, or that you wish you could start over, or that you just can't bear to hear one more "Mommy? I need you!"

Probably many times. But of course they've always reassuringly said, "Oh I know that. You're just tired (or upset, or lonely or frustrated)." You felt better knowing they understood and relieved to have been able to express a seemingly taboo thought, which is, "If only I didn't have my kids I could. . . ." These are musings and feelings with which only other parents can truly identify. Scratch the surface of any delighted mom or dad and you'll find a person who sometimes wishes he or she could escape to Hawaii without the kids for a ten-year vacation.

Let's face it, at times you feel like a trapped animal. And as with most feelings, it's sometimes hard to hide them, especially from the people with whom you live. So, you might as well be prepared to explain to your kids why, for the briefest moments, you have this completely ridiculous fantasy/nightmare that either you could run away or they would disappear even though if they did or you did, you wouldn't want to live another day because nothing in the whole world means as much to you as they do.

Everyone needs to blow off steam from the downside of parenting but when you do it in front of your children, it will hurt them. They may perceive themselves as unworthy and undeserving of loving care. Making a kid feel like a burden (which they sometimes are) is rejecting, frightening (they have to have someone meet their needs because they can't do it all by themselves), and painful to them.

You've been dating a very wonderful guy and while you're not at all sure "this is it" you do desperately wish you had more time to spend with him. Unfortunately for you (and more for your children), your ex, their father, moved too far away to see them every other weekend. You try to get them sleepovers but while this works for your thirteen-year-old, the lively six-year-old isn't always welcome. Parents are tired on the weekend and running after two six-year-olds can be an imposition. One morning, you're on the phone with a friend, complaining, "Sometimes I wish my kids would just disappear. All I want to do is hop on a plane with Dennis and run away." Suddenly you hear something crash to the floor behind you. Whirling around you see your six-year-old has dumped the entire contents of his crayon box on the kitchen floor. "I hate you!" he screams. It's fair to say you feel the same way about yourself.

The first thing you need to do is understand and forgive yourself. The feeling you expressed to your friend is completely normal. Somehow single parents who already feel guilty about what they have visited upon their children think they now have to be super-parents! They have to be able to give, give, give. But this isn't realistic. Parents all over the world sometimes wish their kids would disappear. Maybe they feel they can't afford them, or need time to be alone, or need private time with a spouse. Parents may sometimes think they can't take the emotional responsibility one more minute, or simply that they don't have another molecule to give. The simple fact is single parents need to double, even triple their right to these feelings. You have too much on your plate, and it's very understandable to sometimes want to leave all your responsibilities behind! You're normal and can still consider yourself a wonderful parent.

Of course, as you knew before this happened and are now experiencing in full color, these are not feelings you necessarily want to share with your children. Usually the furthest any of us go is "Leave me alone! I need some private time!" which in the scheme of things is not all that hurtful. You want quiet. You want to be alone to think. It has nothing much to do with your kids except that you want them to give you some space for a while. Sure a younger child might wonder, "Doesn't she like being with me?" but of course that can be handled with adding, "I love you, honey, but sometimes mommies need quiet time just for themselves."

The problem with the overheard conversation is you've gone way beyond the "I want some personal time" remark. You've expressed preferring to be with someone *other* than your child. And you've suggested it might be best if your child just didn't exist. Worse, you might want to leave them!

The most destructive thing you could do is what most parents are tempted to say, which is something along the lines of, "Oh, you misunderstood me." Denying reality is one of the worst things you can do to your child. If they know the truth it will build distrust. If they suspect the truth and you deny it they will grow not to trust their own instincts. It is critical that your children face what they know. It will give them strength and confidence. Turning from or repressing what they know will only engender fear and insecurity and the sense that they don't know what's happening around them. The roots of depression can take hold.

Tell the truth. The whole truth. Your child can take it.

"Honey, I'm so sorry you heard me say that. I know that must have hurt your feelings. I didn't really mean that. I would *never* want you to disappear. But sometimes I would like to just be able to go away and worry only about myself."

"Well, what's the matter with me?" your child might wail (if you're lucky—it's always better if your child can freely express hurt).

"Nothing. I wouldn't change you for the world!" you might say. "Nothing. Not a thing. But I get tired and sometimes I just want to do things that aren't 'mommy things.' Thing that are just for adults." You're hoping he didn't hear the part about Dennis.

"You like Dennis better than me?" he whimpers.

No such luck. *"No, I don't,"* you can say emphatically. "Never more than you. I couldn't love anyone more than you. You are my son."

"But you want to run away!" He's still teary.

At this point you could be wondering if he swallowed a dictation machine.

"I only meant I wanted to go someplace else where I could rest for a while. I enjoy Dennis's company; he's an adult and I wanted an adult vacation that I can't have right now."

Before your son can make another comment, you take over by bringing him back to something to which he can relate. "Remember the other day you had your friend Michael over and I kept coming into your room to put laundry away, or to check on you, or to see what all the loud noises were about."

Jacob nods.

"What did you say? Do you remember?"

He shakes his head.

"You said, 'Leave us alone! Go away!'" You smile at him. "You wanted private kid time. You wanted me to leave. You wanted me to disappear!"

"Not forever," Jacob insists, clearly not wanting to give you more than half an inch.

"Well, that's the same for me!" You grin. "I wanted one of us to disappear so I could be alone with a friend but not forever. Sometimes people feel like that because they have special things they like to do with special people and sometimes they just can't make it happen. So they call a friend and say, 'I wish I could run away,' or they tell their mothers, 'Go away!'"

Jacob will get this. He may smart for a little while longer, but sooner or later he will allow himself to know what he knows. You said some hurtful words, but you love him very much.

An older child may feel hurt as well, and may not be as prone to discussing it with you. In this case you might want, once you realize he's heard the conversation, to track him down and tell him flat out what you meant. (This is also true of a younger child who simply says, "Leave me alone," in response to overhearing the conversation.)

"Look, I know you overheard what I said to Laurie. I don't want to run away. I don't want you to disappear. It's just that sometimes *I am so tired*, and you know I've been enjoying myself with Dennis and I was fantasizing about getting some time alone with him. It's totally an adult thing. I couldn't love anyone more than you and if you ever disappeared from my life, I'd never be happy again." Here too you can smile and remind him of his own fantasies. "You didn't wish I would disappear or you could run away last weekend when I insisted you get your work done instead of joining the kids at the bowling alley? I know you'd be miserable if I disappeared, but I bet for a second you wished it."

Your adolescent might comment grumpily, "Yeah? Well, try me. It'd be fine with me."

"Right." You might nod and then walk away, saying over your shoulder, "We love each other like crazy."

This will not only confirm your love for him, but let him know that words don't always express true feelings that are deepest and at the core. Sometimes they just express frustration or anger or longing and cloud over what is the most essential vow. Clouds pass over giving way to sun. You know he adores you no matter what he says, and he should know you adore him no matter what words might occasionally escape from your mouth.

Your Ex's First New Relationship: Should We Tell Mom?

It's bad news when children feel that they have to keep secrets about one parent when talking to the other. It confuses and frightens them. What if they slip? Who will get in trouble? Mom, Dad, me? And who will be blamed? The worry and anxiety can grow so large that your children may be unwilling to describe anything about their day with the other parent for fear of disclosing something "bad."

And this of course is the other problem. Secrets always take on a "bad" quality. After all, if it was good, why does one have to stay silent? So now you have a child who thinks one parent could possibly be doing something wrong and thus feels extremely protective.

And then finally, your child, viewing you as vulnerable, may be afraid to mention things that could hurt. This is lovely and means your child is growing up and has true heart. But he or she also has too much responsibility and needs to see you as one who is stronger and doesn't need her protection.

Your child is maintaining a good relationship with her father, your ex. She sees Jim every week but the regular visits have softened her feelings of abandonment. You also get a break on an afternoon and weekend with time to yourself. You planned it nicely and so far so good. But then one afternoon, Rose returns late Sunday afternoon and says she wants to play the exact piano recital that she has played for "Dad and . . ." The hesitation is so long you can hardly stand it. "I forget," she finishes. Your stomach clutches; you know it's another woman. Of course, he has every right to have another woman, just as you have every right to have another man. Your head tells you this but your gut is hollering something else. "I've been replaced!" You knew this was going to happen. It had to. It's not that you want your ex back either. No. Not at all. But still, he has found someone to be with and you haven't yet. You want to cry.

Then you pause and consider what just happened. Your very intuitive eight-year-old daughter was keeping a secret. She was trying to spare you something that she sensed would cause you pain. She's probably in a terrible quandary. You *do not* want her to feel this amount of responsibility for something she neither caused or can do anything about.

You take a deep breath. "It's okay, Rose," you say. "If Dad has a new friend (you don't have to say "girlfriend") you can say her name."

Rose becomes uneasy. "But Dad told me not to." You feel annoyed that your ex is asking your child to keep a secret from you. But, you think, maybe he's trying to protect your feelings, maybe he still likes you and doesn't want to make you angry, maybe this, maybe that. One thing is for sure though, he's putting Rose in the middle.

"Rose, I know that Dad sees other people and that is fine. I don't want you to take responsibility for trying to protect me from knowing things like this. You are my girl, and it's unfair for you to be put in the middle. I'm an adult and I don't think it's a good idea for children to have to keep secrets. I'll mention it to Dad and I'm sure he'll agree. He was probably just uncomfortable for a minute and didn't think about it much."

"Okay," Rose says and starts plunking out "Yellow Submarine" on the piano.

You really don't want to hear about your ex's girlfriend, but it is inappropriate for your child to take this responsibility for you and your ex's feelings. Recognizing this is healthy parenting.

But it's also healthy parenting to clarify the way in which you will handle these kinds of situations with your ex. The two of you do need to come to an understanding about what to tell Rose concerning the things she witnesses in each of your homes. Certainly she can be told it isn't necessary to share every detail of every conversation that takes place. But it would spare her a lot of internal conflict if she knew that she could share the big things . . . the things that matter to her . . . and which not to talk about would leave her feeling unhappy, confused, and afraid "of slipping."

Of course besides telling her what she can do, you have to walk the walk. When she tells you something that hurts, it's important to deal with *her* feelings and save yours for the privacy of your own room, where a good cry, call to a friend, or pounding of a pillow will ease your own emotions.

Not in Front of the Kids (Again?!)

Can you fight with your boyfriend in front of your kids?

Your children have certainly learned that all does not go smoothly in matters of love and relationships. It's likely they heard a great deal of fighting during the last year or so of your marriage. Probably they've felt the tension, seen the grimace on your face, listened to doors slamming, or endured eerie silences.

Then the divorce happened and they found out what the noise was all about.

The question is, what have they concluded from this? That conflict can be dangerous? That only couples headed for divorce or separation have dramatic arguments or creepy coldness between them? That people who no longer love each other fight loud? That if someone abruptly leaves the table, or slams a door, or shouts "Don't speak to me!" that the relationship is over?

You'd better hope not. Not only is this because you want them to take any arguing they might witness between you and your significant other with some equilibrium, but also you want them to know that when they start dating, arguments can happen and don't necessary spell doom for a relationship.

Of course there is the issue of haven't they had enough?

And the answer is probably yes.

The trick is to display (at least in front of them) a way to argue that still illustrates the presence of love or affection.

You and your boyfriend, Steve, are sitting at the dinner table with your six- and nine-year-old when suddenly Steve announces his buddy has invited him sailing for the weekend and he'd love to go. They used to do it all the time he tells you. The trouble is you've already made plans with another couple and Steve seems to have forgotten. You remind him. "Tell them I'm really sorry," he says blithely. You're ready to chuck the bowl of peas in his lap. You turn to your daughter Ariel, apparently with a look of disbelief and fury

on your face. She looks, for want of a better word, freaked. The silence at the table is deafening.

"What's wrong?" Steve asks, clearly not getting it. "We can reschedule, can't we?"

Of course you can. But you're furious he doesn't seem to have any regard for your friends. You're furious he hasn't asked you if you mind. You're furious he just announced his plans as if no one in the world mattered but himself. You're thinking, "If I wanted to be treated like this I could have stayed married."

However, no matter how you are feeling, it is extremely important that you contain "the scene." The divorce is over, your children may have been through a war zone, and it isn't fair to play it back for them . . . and that *is* how they'll see it. You might say, "I think we should discuss this later when we have a chance to talk alone." Then go about chatting and finishing dinner. The problem with this approach is that chances are the tension will permeate the atmosphere to such a degree that you might as well be fighting.

Your children, having been through conflict already, will likely start feeling anything from nervous to terrified that something terrible is going to happen again. They may want peace and the sense that you two can get along, that men and women *can* be together happily. Of course life is not a fairy tale and your children do have to learn that having survived one divorce does not mean the rest of their and your lives will offer up nothing but daffodils and buttercups. They have to learn that living and fighting goes on. But they also need to see resolutions can be different.

Rather than go for the "later" approach it is better to reach for something in the middle. You can express your negative reactions, so that the air is cleared and your kids can breathe deeply knowing the truth is "out there," but you can also save the details for later. It is highly unlikely that either child will want to hear them. If you and Steve are kissing and snuggling they may (only may) want to peek through the keyhole, but if you're fighting they will probably want to run for the hills.

"Steve, I think we need to talk about this switch in plans. I don't think you've considered everything and I'm a little upset. But now is not the time. Let's do it after dinner when the kids are doing their homework."

When you employ this kind of response you are teaching your children many things:

- You're showing your children you are not afraid to express how you feel.

- Just because you're angry doesn't mean you have to yell and jeopardize a relationship.

- You are confirming reality but controlling fantasy. By acknowledging the tension, your kids will know they've picked up the right signals, but this doesn't have to be a nuclear war.

- You've modeled how to handle a disagreement. Chances are the children didn't see much of that toward the end of the marriage.

- You've made it clear that you want to protect your children from as much unpleasantness as you can and that no argument with your boyfriend is worth making them unhappy.

It is particularly important to keep your cool around young children who will undoubtedly be more shaken up by loud arguing. They will probably fear that once again, someone is going to leave. Remember, they are more frightened of abandonment because they are littler and more dependent. They may start to think that this is how it will always be. A peaceful time, an argument, and *bam,* it's over. It isn't hard to extrapolate from that how such thinking could cause tremendous problems for them later in life. You need to let your children see that an argument handled with respect and fairness can lead to a good, satisfying resolution of a problem. Things *can* be worked out between people.

Conflicts, including ones that are loud and messy, can lead to a deeper understanding and a bond. When emotional feelings and commitments are derailed, you need to model how to get them back on track by dignifying all sets of feelings involved. This involves respectful conversation, compromise, acceptance, and a return to affection. Of course this process in its entirety cannot take place in front of your children, but these underlying values can be brought to their attention as a goal. If your children nervously ask how you and Steve are going to work it out you can say, "We just got into a bad place together and when it cools down, I hope we can talk it out and both feel better. This may take some doing. I have great affection for Steve but it can't work smoothly 100 percent of the time." You might encourage your children to talk about angry feelings that they have had for a grandparent, teacher, or baby-sitter that actually melted into a loving understanding when the hurt quieted down.

Your older children by now probably have some idea that these things happen to people outside of divorces, and that life goes on. They will probably handle an argument a bit more comfortably. But even a teenager is going to be angry. Enough already, he will probably think. And he'll be right.

After you've expressed your feelings in a limited way to your companion, you might want to make a concerted effort to change the subject and concentrate on the children. This shouldn't be too hard. Your children, no matter what age they are, will be grateful for the switch in focus.

Finally, whether or not you resolve the argument peacefully, be sure to tell your companion that he has to leave calmly and that when you cool down, you will try again to work it out. Your efforts will keep the children from being subjected to a dramatic exit that will both upset and confuse them and throw them back to the question that undoubtedly hung in the air during the separation—is he coming back? If indeed the argument is a deal breaker you can talk to them about that later in a calm way explaining your differences. But for now it is critical that you protect your child from any more anger between a man and woman.

This is a time for them to see that sometimes relationships can be happy and that when they run into a problem, there are ways to move through the conflict to a new and even stronger place. This is not a time to underline that when things don't click, the only way out is a disruptive and upsetting split.

When a Relationship Doesn't Last for the Long Haul

It's great when your kids can form a relationship with someone you love. But you and this person may not last and when this happens your child can be left holding the proverbial bag. Certainly occasionally reminding your child that not all romances last, and that he has to remember there may be a time when you and Dan have to say good-bye, will help. But it won't keep your child from feeling disappointed, unhappy, and even abandoned if and when that time comes. There are ways, however, to ease the pain and the experience of yet another loss.

> **"When is Dan coming over to play basketball with me?"** your seven-year-old son, Jeff, wants to know.
>
> You feel caught, as you and Dan finally called it quits about a week ago and you haven't really said anything yet. Dan and Jeff had gotten pretty involved through sports and you haven't had the nerve to break his little heart. "Dan can't really come around now because I'm not dating him anymore. I'm so sorry."
>
> You watch Jeff's lip curl. "It's no fair, he's my friend too."

Your son is right, he did forge a separate relationship with Dan and at your encouragement too. It seemed fine at the time. Jeff's dad lives far away and so they only get together mainly on holidays. He calls every night but Jeff was craving some guy time. Dan was happy to do it. The dad role gave him a opportunity to heal his checkered relationship with his own dad by nurturing your son. It had seemed like such a good arrangement, and it was, until now. In the aftermath of the breakup, you have been avoiding the exploration of your child's feelings. You're still too raw and heartbroken to feel like you can talk it out with Jeff without being irritable or bursting into tears. Your needs are wide open and it makes it difficult to tolerate how much your child needs from you. He's so hurt, too. From the beginning you had doubts about you and Dan being right for each other but now that that reality is here, it has hit you like a ton of bricks. Jeff mushes his cereal looking miserable. Your stomach is in knots.

"I know, it really isn't fair when my relationship ends that yours ends too," you say.

"You're right. I want to play a game with him, can't I call him?" Jeff pleads.

You're face-to-face with a basic truth. When you break up with a boyfriend your children come along for the ride, whether they like it or not. They could become impossibly angry and hurt. They've already faced the fact that they had no control over the divorce, and now this breakup too? You can explain to Jeff that you are sad and upset. "But so am I," he might say. This is good. He needs to express these feelings. His hurt in fact might be so palpable that you might wonder if it's an option for Jeff to have some contact with your ex?

Since you didn't set things up in this fashion, the answer might be yes or no. A lot will depend on what you feel you can handle and the feelings of your ex. But for the future here are some things to think about when considering the possibility of your child having a continuing relationship with a person you have stopped dating.

- As part of your breakup conversation, you and your ex might talk about his relationship with your child and how to ease out of each other's lives slowly.

- Perhaps you can help set up a time for your child and ex so they can talk about the big change that has occurred that will interfere with their friendship.

- Your ex could write a letter or make a call to ease your child's feeling that he wasn't important enough to deserve your ex's attention now that things are over with you.

- You might suggest your child write a letter or send a drawing to your ex so that he or she can feel some sense of closure too.

- If the breakup is mutual and not excessively painful you might explore with your ex the possibility of continuing his relationship with your child that involves some contact between them on a regular but not frequent basis. (You may elect to try this after a month or so has passed and you feel more surefooted about handling the details.)

As for the situation above, though you will likely be in great pain thinking about your ex, and though you would prefer not to keep it in the forefront of your mind, if your child brings him up, stay with it. Then go to your room, close the door, and have a good cry. Your child has been "cut off" from seeing someone he liked. It would be very hurtful for you to cut him off too.

FINDING a meaningful and warm relationship after a divorce is a wonderful thing. But of course it creates dilemmas too. Your needs will often be in direct conflict with those of your children. Everyone needs attention and respect. You might find yourself having to compromise a great deal. But certainly so will your children! The key is to try to create an atmosphere of compassion.

5

Getting Serious:
Do You Love Him More
Than Daddy?

You're in love.

This is the first time you have been in a position to want to go some distance with a partner since your divorce—the aftermath of which left you questioning your trust in love, your belief in forever after, honor, loyalty, responsibility, and healthy obligation.

Life had settled down and now you're about to mix it up again. How in the world will all those "his" and "her" elements find a place in your life? How is it going to feel trading the "I" for a "we" when this time it could be forever? Until now, you could sense other relationships would end. You'd be getting back to the safe though lonely place you had been. But this relationship is different and sometimes so overwhelming in concept that you find yourself worrying about the seemingly smallest things . . . leaving aside the big stuff for a rainy day you hope never arrives. Trying to get a consensus on what movie to rent on a Saturday night can be a long-drawn-out discussion in your house. How in the world are you going to regularly add another opinion to the mix? Your children are used to Friday night Chinese take-out. But he doesn't like Chinese food. What if he can't handle the kind of noise the kids make in the car? They travel loud. The list titled "Make room for David" is endless. After all, how many fingers can be in the same pie in the same house in the same universe when that universe has found its balance—uneasy as it might be and as much as you've wanted it to change?

Of course these minor concerns are really masking the bigger issues that will have to be addressed. Here you are resurrecting hope and faith in front of both your children. This decision to be a real couple amounts to an unscripted journey for you and your family and could be fraught with emotional minefields.

Initially your children may not be able to see anything positive about your relationship with David, believing life is now going to be a giant mess. Or they may fantasize lovely things. Then again they may embrace both possibilities during the course of a single day. Or they could decide it's going to be okay, because what does it matter? It's your life and they'll just ignore it. And you. The one thing they won't spend a lot of time doing is reflecting on how great this change is for you. It's not that they don't want you to be happy. It's just that they don't want it at their expense.

They may be quite healthfully narcissistic about this, with an attendant regression setting in. You will likely have to maintain a sense of humor about it, despite wanting to occasionally scream, *"Doesn't anyone care he makes me happy?"*

You might have thought your children got past their need to blame, be angry, and fantasize a reunion. After all, you've only discussed their feelings with them over the years a thousand times. But there's nothing like you falling deeply in love to inspire a thousand more talks. It's little wonder. Once again it appears that their world is going to dramatically change, and in response, your children may have some of those old (and all too familiar) concerns, and some new ones as well.

Minefield 1: Wanting Your Unit to Stay As Is

They want to be with you but they don't want him to be there too because it just feels different. And it is. Friday nights were a time the three of you always hung out together, often watching a video. Your daughter could wear any old rag T-shirt, lie across your legs, and talk nonstop about the action and characters on screen.

Now, she says that she feels uncomfortable. She resents having to wear more clothing and feels like she might be judged if she makes comments. She's not too far off base. Peter doesn't like a lot of talking during a movie. He also may not realize the necessity of accepting, at least at first, some of your set family rhythms. He may not know how much your child would like to be accepted by him. Until they can experience some commonality and a meshing of humor, any changes Peter brings to family patterns may not be received well. In fact, they may cause mini explosions.

Minefield 2: Guilt over Liking Your Companion

Your children really think your girlfriend is cool and better at art than their mom but they are seized with guilt over these feelings. Kids may feel uneasy about caring for a new person especially if they favor some of the new person's qualities; how can they dare like someone more than Mom or Dad? It could feel like an unmanageable betrayal. But both parents need to encourage children to enjoy, love, and relate to anyone who enhances their life experience in a healthy way even if they have to hold their nose to do it. It's simply in the best interest of the child who is far better off feeling free to enjoy good feelings than being pressured to view new people through a negative prism.

Minefield 3: Fear of the New You

They want to be sure this new person won't change you—knowing full well that you are already behaving differently. They may fantasize being ignored or disliked. After all, already you're more preoccupied than usual. They may wonder about his kids and wonder how you are with them. They may fear the pressure to be someone they are not. This is true especially if you give forth with a barrage of "Now, try to be polite" or "Clear the table after dinner without me asking, okay?" or "Please don't tell any of those baby jokes you think are so silly. They are but I don't think he'd appreciate them." They may fear you will care about him more than them. It will be important to use some old scripts even though the play is changing.

Minefield 4: The Fantasy of Bliss

They may also imagine a Garden of Eden that you and he simply cannot possibly create. After all of the discord and difficult adjustments they are now ready for the cornucopia of family life, which includes all things wonderful. Entertaining dinners, family outings, no more dreary Sunday evenings, and more. Best of all, here's another adult ready to fulfill all of their most unfulfilled desires.

Unfortunately, kids can be extreme sometimes.

Then again so can adults. Sometimes we are all cockeyed optimists. You too undoubtedly have fantasies about how all the people you love will get along. In your mind's eye you can see it all. Occasional spirited outings with all of you laughing and talking together. Dinners during which your children pepper your companion with questions that show their obvious interest and inspire his affection. You might even imagine yourself with his kids, chatting away, only to receive a call late that night from him saying, "They loved you!"

It's a pretty good bet that what happens is going to be a mixed bag. There will be difficult moments that never even occurred to you might happen, pleasures you never dreamed of, and everything in between—over an extended period of time.

Your goal of course will be to help ease your children into accepting this new person as part of their lives. To do this you will want to understand their views and tread very carefully and respectfully as they experience minor changes and then perhaps more significant ones as time passes. The most important thing to keep in mind during this process is that your children did not choose this man. You will do well to minimize your expectations, so that they have a chance to build a relationship on their timetable, not yours.

Can't Hide the Real Feelings

Children are like sponges, picking up the vibes and unconscious meandering of adults' minds. It is right to validate what a child instinctively knows. To do otherwise is to ask them to deny what they can sense is true. Pushing children to doubt and mistrust their correctly perceived reality can make them feel at best confused, and worse, crazy.

If a child says, "I know you like him," or, "Something's going on between you two," denying it serves no healthy purpose. Offering an affirmative and making it clear that you do not wish to talk about it any further for right now is a better choice than trying to snuff out the accurate hunch. Kids need to know they can always ask; otherwise you run the risk that their concerns will go underground and fester. This can do unpredictable and ofttimes destructive things to their inner worlds.

You've been keeping a low profile with Jason. You've done this with all of your boyfriends. He has been over just a few times. You haven't wanted to scare or overwhelm your children. In fact, the closer you and Jason grew the less they saw him. You wanted to be sure before you spoke. And you were also feeling extremely self-conscious. What if your children could tell you were falling in love? Better to keep it away from them and then slowly, slowly introduce the idea.

But there were, you realize now, various information leaks such as a scratched name on a notepad, suddenly an extra night here or there with a baby-sitter, a furtively closed door when the phone rings. They caught on despite your best efforts to shield them.

"We figured it out," your twelve-year-old announces. "You've got a real-life boyfriend," your nine-year-old son chimes in. "It's Jason, right?" They're direct. They're to the point. In fact they are just a tad challenging. You can tell, other than this, they don't quite know how they feel. You suspect, however, that fear is in the mix, and recognizing that what they don't know can give rise to upsetting fantasies, you decide to be as straight about this as you can. After all, the jig is up. But you also keep in mind not to tell them more than they need or want to know. You go step by step.

"Jason is a friend of Arlene's and he is also divorced with a son and daughter," you offer.

"How old?" your son asks.

"Fifteen," you say.

He's disappointed. You suspect he wanted a baseball-obsessed nine-year-old.

Your daughter asks a little shyly what he's *really* like. Does he skate, do you know whether his daughter is cool in any way, and then, not exactly in these words, where exactly is this relationship going? She is almost panicky on this last inquiry as if her life is about to be pulled out from under her. You know you will have to level with her. She is not unlike you when you are faced with a new situation; you get anxious too. So here at the kitchen table is your little mirror in the form of your daughter's wary eyes.

He is, you offer, the first person since you began dating, for whom you feel love. "I'm happy in a special way now. It's like when you meet a new friend and you find that you have a lot in common and really want to 'hang out' and share with them. It's like that." You smile inside, wondering if your children can see how happy you feel.

Then again, what are they really feeling inside?

Most likely they are concerned and on alert. Your behavior with Jason differs from the way you behaved with other men. Certainly you're happier but probably less attentive to them and your children will probably be trying to figure out whether this is good news or bad.

"Yes, I love him."

When your children know through your words and actions that you love someone there will be a decisive emotional shift in how they view your relationship. Love is a big deal. The stakes go way up. Love, they know instinctually, changes everything. It's a deep, strong bond. You certainly have this with them. But now they may start wondering, are you willing to go out on a limb for him as you do for them? And if so, will there still be room on that limb for everyone? Your children will likely become extraordinarily watchful. They will take sharper notice of your comings and goings. And they may grow irritable.

They've seen Jim casually and seem to like him. You've taken it slow. Jim has come in, chatted, joined in here and there, and then left. He's become familiar but not central for them.

Suddenly your daughter asks sharply, "You're seeing Jim again this weekend?" You begin to feel like the teenager who is accountable to the weary parent. Parents are afraid that as their children leave the nest, they will change, become almost unrecognizable, and slowly disconnect from the family. Your daughter is in all likelihood experiencing the same kinds of feelings! She's afraid you'll change. She's afraid you'll "leave the nest." Of course as a parent, you know you would never leave your child behind. But you do have to acknowledge that this new person is someone you love and want to have in your life and, yes, indeed the nest is going to change a bit. Your children will have endless questions about that "love" and where they fit into it.

"Do you love him more than you did Dad?" your nine-year-old wants to know. This is one of those questions children ask when they might really want to know something else. Will you love him more than me? Is Dad going to feel bad when he finds out? I thought you loved Dad forever and it ended. Is this going to end too?

You explain, as you have before, that you loved Daddy so much when you had children but that over time each of you changed, as did your love, and so you couldn't live together anymore. You tell him that the love a parent feels for a child never changes. You assure him that you and his father wish each other happiness and that while each of you might feel a little sadness as the other moves on, it is important to keep living and enjoying the sweet things that life offers. You also add that you have been hoping to find someone with whom you can grow and really stay together forever. You're hoping that you have found this in Jim.

"What if I don't love him?" your seven-year-old asks. He's testing. He wants to know that if he doesn't stay with the program is he on the outs? He is going to need to know this is not an "either-or" proposition. "You are free to have whatever feelings you have," you tell him. You hope that he will come to like this person but you cannot control his emotions nor would you want to. (Pushing something on a child will most likely backfire into some form of opposition.) Finally, it's important to add, "No matter how you end up feeling about each other, honey, I will always love you."

"Will he love me too, Mommy?" your five-year-old wants to know. You love her so much that you figure someone you love will love her too. But of course, you know that this is not always the way it works. "I know he enjoys you lots and I feel that he will love you because you are so wonderful." For a young child an affirmative answer is important. The subtle distinction between enjoying, loving, and liking won't mean much to her. She just wants to be sure she's on the right side of the road.

An older child will be able to handle liking and respect without love more easily than young children who always want to be the center of important adults' lives. She will also know that the fact that you love Jim is an extremely big deal and is bound to affect her.

"Is he going to be here all the time?" your thirteen-year-old winces. You can tell she's really asking whether he will be taking your attention away from her.

"No, not all the time, I still will have plenty of special time with you."

"So, he's not like going to take over or anything?"

You reassure her, "Not at all; he may join in some family activities but that might be fun for you too. We've all had some good times before."

"Yeah, he's okay," she says, "but don't push it, Mom."

Translation? Go ahead and love him, but let me move at my own pace.

No matter what age your children, knowing you love someone is going to give rise to a lot of complicated feelings. They will need to express them. The best way to make sure they keep talking is to make it clear you don't "need" them to feel any particular way. In fact it would even be wise to keep what you would prefer to yourself as well. They will know you would ideally like them to join in the love fest. But at least initially they may not want to hear it.

What's in It for Me?

You are asking your kids to include someone else they don't really know on an outing they usually enjoy alone with you. And it's not just any person. It's someone you love and will want to pay attention to. So really, what's in it for them?

Some children will see this person as a window of opportunity. How they react depends on their relationship with their other parent, and how much they can imagine this person being a boon for them. Your boys may not be getting enough guy time so they may be less threatened by your new love, imagining him able to do the things you won't. Your need to have Tom come along is in sync with their need for male contact, so for the moment, at least on the first outing, things will run smoothly.

For your daughter, a new major player in your life may feel like a terrible betrayal to her father and to the stability, regularity, and equilibrium (more or less) that has taken hold since Dad left. This new person may remind her of the loss of her own father as a constant presence in her life. Yes, maybe there's a hole in the life she has gotten used to, but now it's a familiar hole. She lives with you, she sees her father, she loves and fights with her brothers; the expectations are steady and clear. She's human, and like most humans, she would rather stick to what she knows. Your need for something new is not in sync with her need to keep things as they are.

Your hope is going to have to be that one day your child will see this new person and the changes he brings as a boon instead of a burden. Wasn't that the hope you had too, that someone would finally come along who was appealing enough to make it worth letting down your guard and loving again? No one wants to give anything up unless there really is something in it for them.

Can You Be Yourself When You're All Together?

You are not only in a new stage of your life, but you're literally on stage too.

You are so very aware of all of those young eyes upon you. They are looking for signs that *you* are going to be different. And truthfully, chances are you will be. When he's around, you find yourself acting a little kinder, moving things more gracefully, and eating less with your fingers. Your kids are bug-eyed as you sashay out of the kitchen with a platter of donuts. What happened to just keeping them in the box? They liked licking their fingers and scraping the box corners for the sprinkled sugar. Is that out now too because of him? And what about the nervous glance you shoot toward this new person each time he speaks with your kids? Clearly, you are weighing how he is receiving their comments.

When he's around, you may be more on or more irritable, more formally dressed or faux casual, or anything from more relaxed to unusually uptight. Hopefully things will even out into a new "normal" pattern, but right now as you are all feeling your way, the changes might seem (and may in fact be) more extreme.

All these modifications, though not vast, add up. This could, for your children, initially be quite upsetting. You used to hang on their every word. But now you have to also hear someone else's. You may seem less attentive. Less involved. You used to laugh at their noise. But now it seems to grate on your nerves . . . especially when he's around. Before you could get quiet. Down. But now, suddenly, you sparkle.

The day begins normally on this sunny Sunday. Everyone gets dressed in their rooms. Jay annoys Beth and you hear her tell him to knock it off once or twice. An ordinary day. You feel excited to see Tom and when the doorbell rings, you move perhaps a bit too fast past your daughter toward the front door. "That must be him," you say. She looks at you. "Wow, you're never that happy when we walk in. . . ." And then her eyes travel down. "Button your top button, it's too low."

Ah, sexuality. Your daughter doesn't want you to have any. Not now anyway. You leave your clothing as is; you've been wearing this shirt in front of her in exactly this fashion for a year. "It works for me; I've always worn it this way," you say, in as kind and low-key a voice as you can muster. One thing you don't need right now is a power struggle, nor do you want to dress like a seminary student at your daughter's command. You add, in order to help her relax, a compliment. Reaching out, you touch her blouse. "That color looks great on you." This strategy works. "You got this for me." She smiles in spite of herself. Crisis averted . . . temporarily.

Vive la Différence

There might be times when that fact, not being the mother you used to be, is a gift to you and your children. Maybe not being your old self is a boon. Single parents and children can come together in very intense ways—very dependent ways. The introduction of someone new can loosen those ties and give everyone permission to see situations and each other differently. Initially your children may be resentful that you are not acting quite like yourself, but after a while they might actually enjoy it.

You're sitting in the restaurant with your restless children chatting away with Tom. Suddenly seven-year-old Jay stands up and asks to go the men's room. You can see the entrance from where you sit. But that's little comfort to you. "Sure," you say. "I'll wait outside the door." But then Tom puts his hand on your arm and says, "He's a big boy. He can handle it. I'll check on him if it takes too long." Jay stares at him with wonder. And then with a cocky grin he walks himself over to the facilities.

And then he comes back, safe and sound. "Good going," Tom says.

Jay glows.

Had you been on your own this wouldn't have happened. You'd have been more uptight. More protective. Instead you let Jay enjoy some independence.

Yes, you're different, and it's great.

Gauging if It's Too Much Togetherness

The best barometer as to "how much togetherness is too much togetherness" is your children. Certainly you will want to start off slowly. Suddenly inviting a stranger into your lives each and every day is going to be very uncomfortable if not downright painful for your children. But going slow (or at least what you think is slow) and building is no protection against hurting them either. Chances are you are operating on very different time clocks. In the end both of you will have to stop and synchronize.

Your children's behaviors will speak volumes. Your job is to stay watchful. Some children who need to pull back into their old life before him will tell you, "I don't want him to be there" or "It's just for you, I don't want you to share it with him." If only life were so simple. Other children will become moody or irritable, and start displacing emotions like anger onto people or things. If your seven-year-old suddenly hates his favorite dinner meal, snapping, "I'm sick of this. I hate it!" take note. Angry outbursts at previously benign events or unusual fights with friends are pretty strong clues that something else is going on.

One ten-year-old who really enjoyed her dad's partner and looked forward to their outings would completely tighten up physically if her mother happened to be attending the same event in their community. "You could tell she just couldn't handle it well," her dad said. "She'd stop talking to me and Joan and stand three feet away; talk about body language! We try to avoid those situations—it's not great for her or for us."

One couple waited to bring their kids into the mix until they had achieved a really good comfort zone in their partnership. They knew each other well and thankfully had some nonverbal communications to rely on when the kids were around. A look from each other could help soothe and smooth the rough patches that occasionally erupted.

After maybe two months, Jerry became a regular visitor. He was around several days a week, often helping the kids with their homework or hanging out to watch a video. You had stopped thinking twice about inviting him to join in family activities with you and your two girls. You were feeling quite good about things, and in fact your girls seemed particularly happy to roll with whatever weekend plans evolved. Or so you thought.

It's Sunday evening, Jerry has just gone home, and you are forced to realize things are not quite as rosy as you had thought. Your fifteen-year-old says in an annoyed tone, "Jerry's here an awful lot." You lift an eyebrow and she says nothing more. You're tired of exploring every nuance of every feeling she has and so this time you just don't. She gets along beautifully with Jerry. She knows it and you know it. You figure whatever is going on will blow over.

However, on Wednesday evening, Jerry and his two sons join you and the girls at a pizza joint. The girls usually see their dad on Wednesdays but at the last minute, he got stuck on some assignment at his office and begged off.

Later, at home, Kelly begins carping that she is tired of having to be in on your new life. Just because Jerry means so much to you doesn't mean she wants to have to eat meals with him and his kids all the time. She's working her way into a rageful mood, which is unusual.

It's true that you have been giving yourself more freedom in your relationship with Jerry. For a couple of years after the divorce, your focus was your children and their grieving and adjusting to this monumental change. But now, you take more time away from them and also include your romantic life in their lives. You take Kelly seriously but also feel annoyed at having to be sensitive in the face of her blazing anger. What does she want from you? Finally you are no longer lonely. You flash on your therapist friend who said that it is important not to give kids "too much power and control." That may be true. But are you changing in ways that are too hard for your child to handle? Are you expecting too much togetherness?

You force yourself to sit down and sympathetically say, "Kelly. What's going on here? I know you like Jerry. And maybe it has been too much. Tell me what's bothering you exactly." Fortunately Kelly is willing to talk. (If she hadn't been you would have had to try again later . . . if just to prove your sincere interest in wanting to help her.) As you listen, you realize that Kelly is really angry at her dad for letting her down. In the old days, when Dad bowed out, Kelly could have all of you to herself and so her disappointment was absorbed by the undivided attention you gave each other. In this case, she felt adrift and created a conflict based on the notion that Jerry was supposed to be replacing her father for the evening . . . and that wasn't going to fly. You acknowledge her sadness by saying, "You miss your father. That's a big deal." She eases up on being angry. "I know this is different than it used to be. Here you are sharing Dad with work and then having to share me with Jerry and his family." Kelly is also becoming more conscious of the fact that Jerry is really in her life and very important in your life and that her father will never have his same place in this family. It is very hard to accept the loss.

As much as you love Jerry and hope that your future will be bright, you need to remember new dynamics are created by a new person. Whether these dynamics are good or bad, your children will certainly experience them as unfamiliar, and probably not in a very happy light, until they know your mate better. If conflicts continue to arise with your children telling you in the many ways available to them (tantrums, storming away, nasty comments, deadly silences, tears, and accusations) that it's just too much too soon, listen to them. They should not be required to go along with every plan because you need them to. They do need some decision-making power. It is true they can't be given full control. But they ought to be given some . . . if not simply because it's the surest road to them being, in the future, able to relinquish it.

Not Every Person Will Be Great with Your Kids

In a perfect world, your new love would be remarkably skilled at entering your kid's lives. With grace and ease, he would pass all the tests, avoid all the pitfalls, and if necessary, climb every mountain. What a lovely dream.

Some of the most well-intentioned people can be real clinkers with your kids. First of all, they don't know them and are walking into a den of need, suspicion, and nonchalance that comes in packages of all ages, histories, sexes, and personalities. A decathlon might take less strength. And don't forget how awkward this can be for you. You've been relating to your kids in a certain way for years and now find yourself under the watchful eye of someone who means a great deal to you but who has never really seen you move in this context. Maybe he will admire the choices typical of your parenting style or maybe he will see you as too lax and indulgent. Even couples having children together for the first time don't know whether their approaches to parenting will be in or out of sync with one another. Remember wincing when you watched your ex handle some act of discipline? Back then you could probably discuss it with a degree of ease. And chances are you'll get to that place with your new companion as well. But it's an educational process for everyone. You have to learn what you can expect. He has to find out who your children are. Both of you have to recognize each other's limitations and step in to fill the holes. And most important, each of you has to allow the other to stumble.

After all, kids can trip up the most connected, loving, and available parents. All they have to do is want to!

First there is the issue of temperamental fit. Even when you have biological children, there is no guarantee that you and your child will, figuratively speaking, be made for each other. An adventurous mom could have a reticent, shy child. This is a combo ripe for problems (though surmountable ones).

One very laid back, soft-spoken mother had a second child, a boy, who was nothing short of rambunctious. She was exhausted trying to parent him because her own natural style was so different. Her first boy was artistic and less active, and parenting him had been a breeze. She had expected the same experience with her second one. "It's a major challenge figuring out the best way to support his nature and not have it be too overwhelming and abrasive to the way my own energy is. I guess it's a life lesson." She laughed. "I let my husband take over a lot with him."

This same concept holds true for a partner that you bring into your children's lives. Sometimes they will hit it off with relative ease and sometimes, divorce issues and conflicts not withstanding, they will not be a great match.

You adore your new partner. Paula is an excellent combination for you. You are cautious socially, she moves with grace and skill through all kinds of gatherings. This has resulted in you getting out more and her helping you to comfortably ease into new settings. She breaks the ice and in short order you're able to shine in your own way. An extrovert and a doer, her energy has added a zest to your life.

However, your son, Jake, who is fourteen, is closer to your temperament and is used to quiet outings with you. You love him dearly and have been content to work on projects like building a shed in the backyard or landscaping the garden without being too talky with one another. Somehow being together and sharing an activity has been the way for the two of you; it has its own kind of closeness and intimacy.

Enter Paula. Though she has been apprised of Jake's style and certainly is familiar with yours, their energy match is off. She is careful to tone down her forwardness, but when Jake is around her, he becomes even quieter. This makes her want to question him more as a way to establish some kind of connection. When Paula is around, Jake is polite in a perfunctory kind of way but goes off into his room with his friends. This teen clan behavior is normal but it's also quite pointed. Paula, who does not have children of her own, often feels hurt. When that happens she herself retreats and then the two of them seem to end up as reluctant sparring partners each in their corner of the ring.

You certainly don't want to give Paula up because you feel more awakened and alive than you have in years, but the communication between Paula and Jake has become stilted and painful. This is also hard for Paula, who loves you but did not want to sign on to a personality excavation in order to have a relationship with your child. Actually, she had been looking forward to a lively interaction with Jake. She's terribly disappointed.

The first step is for you and Paula to realize there will be no quick and easy solution. Both Paula and Jake have to give one another time to find those deeper aspects of each other's personality that can connect. These areas of mutual interests and beliefs are undoubtedly there. The second step is to not push so hard. Pushing reticent people only makes them dig their heels in more.

Perhaps Jake, you, and Paula can find a new side-by-side activity to enjoy in a parallel way. This, after all, is what Jake is used to. Interaction could come out of negotiating—will it be the ski slope, the concert hall, or the planning of where shrubs should be planted? Paula, being the adult, will have to take the biggest step in adjusting her expectations and natural tendencies to be "out there," especially in the beginning. But Jake needn't be left "off the hook." At age fourteen, Jake is in the process of coming out of the self-absorbed trance of childhood to a more related and empathic set of skills needed to be a healthy adult. He can be reminded that his behaviors will have an impact on others. Though you can certainly acknowledge that he and Paula are different, it is good practice for him to also understand the feelings of another person, recognize the differences, and find a way to enjoy and appreciate her (as his Dad does).

Your partner may be awkward with children, not have a major interest, expect too much, be too critical or really too loose, and generally be at a loss. These relationships that are not natural fits may never be great but through talking and awareness they can be made more workable and kindhearted. Who knows what feelings can develop when a proper seed is planted and fed with good intentions and care? Sincerity and stick-to-itiveness can prevail and even triumph. "I couldn't stand her at first but now I realize she's okay" may be music to your ears.

And what if you can't make headway with his children? This is bound to be frightening to you. What, after all, must your new companion be thinking? Do his kids see something about you he doesn't? Are you going to ruin his time with them? Will he want to see you less?

The best thing to do is bring your concerns out in the open. Certainly you don't have to say, "Jimmy hates me. Are you going to start hating me too?" But a comment such as "I think Jimmy is unhappy when I'm around. What do you suggest I do? I was thinking . . ." And then describe the position you'd like to take. This will convey your sensitivity to his son's feelings, and your own desire to work things through with his father's input. Then, no matter what, don't try so hard. Observe who this boy is with attention to what he might need and could be thinking. Don't fake affection. But extend genuine interest. Be consistently kind and available when he appears open to your input. Try a little humor. If you and Jimmy have yet another tense moment in a short period of time, you might try smiling and say, "Boy, it gets icy in here sometimes, doesn't it? What *are* we going to do about it?"

His answer might be flip, but even so, informative. "You could leave," rude as it is, could open the door to a discussion about why he resents your presence. You'll be on your way to a pattern of honest communication. That has to lead somewhere positive.

Navigating the New Lay of the Land

You can't possibly anticipate all the combinations of dynamics that will arise in your new household. Your best preparation is to accept that at any given moment your children may create mundane, complicated, or even creative tangles.

You, Jim, and your kids are all excited to be getting away for a beach weekend. It's the first time you've all been away together. You and Jim have been a couple for over eight months, and he has logged many hours with your kids . . . even attending your thirteen-year-old's debate team event. The man is a prince. He deserves the sound of ocean waves washing over him. Besides, this is going to afford serious bonding time for the four of you. Lucy, your thirteen-year-old, has even agreed to baby-sit one of the nights for Victoria, her eight-year-old sister, so that you and Jim can go out. Friday evening, you all take off in the car.

It's late when you arrive, and you are all ready to sack out. Unfortunately your children are creatures of habit. Victoria wants to sleep in the same bed with you as she almost always does when you go on a trip. You explain to her that it's different this time now that Jim is with you.

"Please, just for this one night," she begs.

"She always does this when we go away." Lucy looks at her sister and rolls her eyes. It's unclear to you whose side she's on. You suspect she doesn't know how she feels. Jim raises an eyebrow and you feel like a complete fool for not having thought to talk this out with Victoria yesterday. Now what do you do in the eleventh hour?

Who sleeps where can be a big deal when you still have young children who have gotten used to climbing into bed with you. A significant other can change this arrangement in a flash and your child's hurt or anger will very likely ignite!

It's definitely a judgment call here. Victoria is eight. She is at an age where she can share, understand reason, and grapple with changing circumstances. She is able to catch glimpses outside just her world. Had she been any younger it would have been harder to expect her easy compliance. A "no" from you might have been felt as a flat-out rejection and led her to a "Jim is more important than me" conclusion. It would have been wise in that case to allow her to spend that first night or part of the night (until she fell asleep, having made that clear to her) in your bed and hope the living room sofa is comfortable.

But Victoria is eight and you decide that it is okay to set a boundary. You and Jim are a couple for these nights. "Jim is here with us and we are sharing my room, when we travel together," you say gently.

"But just one night with me?" Victoria begs, really, truly not wanting things to change for her.

So you go for a compromise. "I will come in and cuddle with you in your bed before you go to sleep all of the nights."

"You're mean," she says.

"I'm not doing it to be mean; you girls go up to your room and get ready for bed, I'll be up in a few minutes." You are holding steady. Victoria stomps off, wounded but you can tell without permanent damage. Lucy follows not saying much of anything. You keep your promise, read to Victoria, kiss her good night and let her know that you are sorry that you hadn't talked this over with her before you all left for the weekend. Your message here is that her feelings are important to you, that she has had to accept a change that she wasn't expecting, and that you appreciate all she feels, including her cooperation.

Then you move to the bed of your probably slightly confused adolescent. Her silence, you realize, in no way means she's unconcerned or content or in complete control of the situation. "Honey," you whisper. "I know this is different. I should have thought to talk about it before we left. I love you guys, but Jim and I are going to spend the nights together on this vacation. If you need me just knock. I love you very much."

You don't need to offer any explanation as to *why* you are sharing a bedroom. "We love each other," a seemingly innocuous statement, could be heard as "more than I love you." So keep it simple. If you're asked why, say, "Because that's the way we want it and you both have very comfortable beds and you belong in them. Tomorrow we'll all be together," and then take your leave.

Not Your Home, Home on the Range

As you spend more and more time with your partner's children, you will witness the way he sets down boundaries and rules (or doesn't set them down) and this will arouse all kinds of feelings in you. Maybe you will recall your own childhood memories of having someone tell you when and where you could do things, maybe you are secretly relieved that you don't have to be the one calling the shots and having all kinds of resistance flying your way, or maybe you know that you would do things differently . . . maybe even better. But you try to stay out of it. These kids are not yours and you feel overall that this really is not your domain. Still, it's hard not to be more and more involved as your interactions become more frequent and complex. . . .

Jerry has invited you for dinner on Thursday thinking he will arrive as usual at seven-thirty. You're planning take-out. Scott, fourteen, and Dana, eleven, are home when you arrive. They report their father just called and said he wouldn't be getting home until 8:00. He'd call you just as soon as he could get a break from the emergency meeting at work. You are surprised but make yourself at home as you usually do, having spent a lot of time here over the past year. Dana comes in and out of the living room making small talk. Scott wanders in and you casually ask if he's done his homework and if he needs help. You know from his father that he's been slacking off. This is married life all over again; the kids around on a weekday night, you reading the paper, and waiting for their "other" parent to get home. It feels pleasantly familiar.

The phone rings and Scott yells, "I've got it." Minutes later he comes in and says that he is going over to a friend's house, then to a concert, but not to worry because he completed tomorrow's assignments so everything's cool. It is pretty obvious that both you and Scott know his father would probably not grant permission for him to go out during the week. This is why Scott stands before you in the living room, waiting a bit hesitantly, but clearly ready to bolt before you have serious time to think.

You are in an awkward position. You are not the parent but you are the only adult in charge at this moment. From a kid's point of view, you might win a lot of points and be a really good guy if you just went ahead and said, "Sure, go on, have a good time." But your gut tells you that's not an option.

"Try your father," you suggest. "Maybe they can call him out of the meeting. I don't feel comfortable giving my okay on a school night. I'm not your parent." That last remark is an important one. You are telling him that you are trying to be nothing more than an adult. This will hopefully cut him off at the pass should he have planned to give you the "You're not my mother" routine.

Of course while it's true you're not Scott's parent, you are thrust right into the parenting role. You feel annoyed with yourself for not anticipating that sooner or later your continued presence around your partner's children would have brought you to this moment. However, the evening rules, or any other for that matter, were never discussed between the two of you.

Scott accepts your advice but his father is unavailable. And so, despite the risk of being despised, you tell him that he cannot go. Predictably, Scott is upset. You're upset too but at least you knew to expect it. Any teenager, trying to get away with something while a parental figure is away, would probably put up a fight. Scott is about to stomp out of the room when he suddenly turns and snaps, "You are not my mother, and you can't tell me what to do." And then he glares and waits; he does not flee.

You pause and then reply evenly, "Scott, I'm the one who told you I'm not your parent. But I am an adult. And I have to make the decision I think is right." He may, you realize, storm out of the house and you certainly know you won't try to stop him but the thought upsets you. Fortunately, he rushes off to his room and slams the door. Now what?

It's a little late but not too late to have a talk with Jerry so that you are familiar with the ground rules in his home. You might also discuss what role you can assume if he is not in the home when a decision has to be made. These conclusions must then be shared with the children, with you present, so that any questions or grievances can be dealt with right then and there. Some kids are even old enough to be in on working out a plan.

Younger kids will probably not have the ability to be reasonable. They will need to be told in no uncertain terms, that if you're alone with them, they have to listen. They may agree but then spin out of control when you make a decision they're convinced their parent would not have reached. In this case all you can do is say, "I'm sorry. This is how I feel. When your dad gets back we can discuss it. I'm happy for you to tell him what happened and how you feel." In this way the children won't be able to cast you as the "wicked stepmother" who is doing something dastardly behind their father's back (such as planning to lose them in the forest!). Permission to be open says, "I have nothing to hide. I'm willing to hear another view and we'll all go from there."

Can't it Just Be Us for Once?

We are all sensitive to being included or excluded. In the fifth grade when you weren't invited to a particular party, you surely experienced a pang of feeling left out. If two people at the office go out to lunch, you may wonder why you're not invited even though you don't really want to go. Now you are an adult included enough of the time to be confident and satisfied. But feeling "left out" is not age limited.

It's your girlfriend, Jan's, birthday on Wednesday and you have a lovely celebration planned. On Saturday, there is another gathering with Jan, her parents, and her two daughters. You have left the date open since you actually like all of these people and are looking forward to seeing everyone. But Jan calls on Thursday to ask you if it would be all right if you don't attend the party. Lynda, fourteen, just wants to be with her grandparents, who she hasn't seen in a long time, along with her mother and sister. "Are you okay with this?" Jan asks. "With the week we all took together last month, I think Lynda is feeling like pulling back and I don't want to push her on this. What do you think?"

Suddenly you're back in fifth grade.

Certainly you know your beloved is probably trying to give her daughter much needed room to breathe. Jan goes on to tell you that Lynda spoke about not feeling like she could totally be herself when you are around. Even though she really likes you, which she has voluntarily shared with her aunts (who told Jan), she sometimes just wants to go back to the way things were with only the three of them or with just the immediate family. "Maybe she needs to touch home base the way it was," Jan explains.

You begin to realize it's not so easy putting yourself in the shoes of an adolescent who has one foot in a child's world and the other in an adult's.

Jan, you realize, loves you and doesn't want to hurt you by asking you to absent yourself from the party. But she's caught and is leaning toward giving Lynda her way since you have all been together so much over the last months. She wants you to be okay with it.

Fighting down your initial inner feeling of "Why can't I go too?" you realize you have to be fine with it. Lynda is fourteen and she wants her mom in the way she used to have her mom along with her grandparents. You and Jan decide you will talk to Lynda to let her know that you understand she wants this experience with just her immediate family. It's important to bring this issue out in the open because to pretend this decision was not a measured one would hide it from everyone's conflicted feelings. "I really appreciate your not being mad at me," she blurts out. It's rather charming and mature of her and so you assure her that you are nothing of the kind.

Of course it's important when making such judgment calls that no one give a child too much power and control. In this particular situation, Jan felt that there had been a lot of time spent together and that Lynda's request felt genuine and understandable. Younger children will often, when given a little room, reach for a lot more with no apparent reason. This is where giving in too often can be a problem. If you stay very aware of each circumstance you should be able to tell the difference between an urgent need to be alone with a parent and a merely frivolous one. A young child who wants to throw pots at the local studio just with you "because we like art so much together!" is a far different request than a youngster who insists your girlfriend stay home while you go to the annual Memorial Day parade where he will be ignoring you and running around with his chums anyway.

The truth is, sometimes when you grant a request, it actually reduces that person's need to control under different future circumstances. And given the way that Jan's girls greet you a week later, you have a feeling that your willingness to back off did a great deal for their ability to trust you . . . and your intentions. You are in no way trying to detract from their time—or relationships—with Mom.

Of course, there may be times when you see your partner as going too far to accommodate her children. Get it right on the table if you genuinely think the concessions are out of whack. Be clear but not critical. "I feel" statements help. They say at once that this is simply how you feel and it's not a question of right and wrong. "I'm not feeling great about always going to a kiddy restaurant on Saturday night. Your daughter can find something good at the Italian place. I want her to have her way and feel good too but I don't think it has to be every time." If your partner resists, just say it would be good for her daughter to share more often. Introducing the concept of consideration for everyone's feelings and needs is healthy and allows children to move beyond their egocentric behaviors.

Kids Need Jobs, or Do They?

Parenting styles and values can vary between two people even when they love each other very much. In the best of circumstances each will learn something from the other and gentle positive changes will occur in each of their styles. But the process can get quite dicey. . . .

> You and your steady companion, Max, are sitting at the dinner table with your two sons, Daniel and Andrew. You've always known that Max has more conservative and stricter notions about how to bring up children (his are already out of the house) but you've never discussed how that might affect interactions with your children. Eleven-year-old Andrew has been after you for months to buy him a new skateboard. "Let's see what your second quarter report card looks like," you offer evenly. "If all your homework is in and there are no complaints from your teacher, we can see about that."
>
> "Why doesn't he try to get a job?" Max asks.
>
> "I walk Laurie's dog," Andrew says. "But that's money for my everyday stuff, so I don't have to ask Mom."
>
> "So why don't you split the skateboard with your mother?" Max continues. "Earn it with good grades and a little work?"

You look across the table at your two sons, who are staring at you uncertainly. This isn't what they're used to. You've been pretty relaxed about satisfying their desires. Certainly you haven't given into everything. But Andrew is dying for that skateboard and good grades *would* be enough for you.

Still, you don't want to simply cast aside Max's suggestion. It would diminish him in front of the boys, and besides, it has some merit.

One concern you will have in this kind of situation is making sure your kids don't see you as suddenly acting completely differently to please your boyfriend. They will become angry and resentful, concluding that you no longer care about how they feel.

Max, they will believe, comes first. Worse still, they may believe you are a traitor.

The second obvious concern is giving Max's suggestion the respect and thought it deserves so that he doesn't feel as if he is a nonentity in your children's eyes or yours. The fact is, an intelligent, caring adult with new perspectives can be beneficial to your family and more specifically to your relationship with your children. Single parenting can sometimes result in patterns and decisions that are not necessarily the most positive for children. The natural need to minimize conflict, which is precisely what a single parent most craves, can result in too few rules and expectations. The need to compensate for the loss of an intact family also enters the decision-making mix.

This situation requires three different conversations. The first is the one at the table. The second is the one with your kids when you're alone. And the third is when you and your boyfriend can steal some private time.

Nodding at your boyfriend, you might say, "That's an interesting idea. Usually during the school year though, the money they earn goes for treats in town, or renting a movie. That kind of thing. Their allowances only pay for essentials—bus passes, lunches, and after-school snacks with friends. But of course the skateboard is a big-ticket item. . . ."

"Mom!" Andrew cries out indignantly.

"Relax," you say softly. "I'm just saying Max has a good point. It is expensive and it might not be a bad idea for you to contribute something toward it. We should talk about this more later." You smile at your son lovingly. "Don't worry. I'm not going to leave you with an empty bank."

Later that evening after Max has gone home you can sit down with the children and have a heart-to-heart about what just happened.

"Listen, guys, obviously Max brought his kids up differently than I am raising you. It doesn't make him wrong and me right, or vice versa. In fact, I have a feeling we all have a lot to learn from each other."

"I think he's mean. I can't earn that skateboard! It's too much. You never would have said that, ever!" Andrew cries out and you're glad of it. He's put all his cards on the table.

"You're right, I wouldn't have," you admit. "But I've been alone with you guys for a while and sometimes I've made choices that might not have been the best for you just to avoid arguments. I mean, what is so terrible about the idea of you contributing to such an expensive gift? It shows you're mature enough to do your part."

"But half?" Andrew is near tears now. "That's a lot of money."

"No, not half. Just something. Let's say 25 percent of the price not including tax, along with good grades?"

"You just want to do what Max thinks is right," fourteen-year-old Daniel says with disgust. "That's pathetic." You know Daniel has been struggling with Max's presence. He was used to being the main guy in the house.

There is truth in what he says—but you want to approve of you also, and you haven't always when you've given in too easily. "Actually, Daniel, I have in the past thought about asking you fellas to see if you could earn a few dollars to help pay for some of the things you'd like. Max's suggestion has just underlined those feelings I've had all along. But I'm not Max either. I think splitting it *is* too much. Some contribution seems exactly right."

Max and Daniel look at you warily. They clearly aren't sure they buy it.

Don't try and convince them. You said your piece. It makes sense. They'll learn as time goes by that you will not forsake them for Max. They may even find that on occasion Max influences *you* to lighten up. Just move on and the truth will soon make itself clear.

Finally, you might want to speak to Max and gently suggest that at least for now he first share his parenting ideas with you alone. You can explain you've been operating differently, though not always effectively. You are very open to his ideas, but you don't want the children to think you have turned over parental decision-making powers to Max. It will make them resent both of you, or at the very least blame him for decisions they don't like. That would make it extremely difficult for the three of them to forge a warm relationship. You might even take the opportunity to give him a few tips on handling your kids. "You don't know them as well as I do," you could remind him.

"So I'm just supposed to shut up when I think something?" Max says a bit testily.

"No," you answer quickly, a bit surprised by how offended he sounds, "but maybe you can come on a little less forcefully. For instance it might have been less provocative for the kids if you'd said, 'Andrew, why don't you also contribute something to the skateboard. You're a big guy. You can make a few dollars.'" You pause. "That kind of thing." You grin. "Flatter him a little too. He likes being a big kid."

Max may shrug but chances are since he cares about you, he'll give it some thought.

Apart As One

It is very painful to watch an evening that was supposed to be a brief merging of both your families turn into a war or "ignore" zone. It's quite common for children, especially when they are expected to feel a certain way about a new relationship, to want to look in the other direction. There's too much pressure in a situation they haven't chosen with unfamiliar kids.

If you're going to plan an evening, you have to be prepared for anything.

If it turns into a love fest, don't expect a repeat performance. There is an artificial quality to these gatherings and it will take time for genuineness to creep in. This process usually involves a fair amount of hurt, confusion, misunderstanding, and resentment. Once resolved, however, your families will be well on their way to becoming "together as one" . . . when the kids are in the mood.

It's family night. Or rather, families night. You and Ted have decided to bring the kids together for a Sunday evening dinner at your home

and an hour or two of hanging out. Your children, Joe, age fourteen, and Marissa, age eight, are not too excited about this. Neither are Ted's two children, Lia, age fourteen, and Sandra, age seven. But the two of you decide it's time.

Dinner goes well enough. There isn't a lot of conversation at the table but the kids talk a little bit to each other about high school, a recent action movie, and beading. You and Ted have to keep the flow going, but you manage.

Then comes hang-out time, and things go mildly haywire. Joe and Lia don't want to be in the same room. Joe wants to watch an old Jackie Chan movie and Lia just wants to read a magazine in the room with you and Ted. Marissa and Sandra are together but arguing fiercely over beads and hemp and who gets what color.

It feels perfectly awful. "There has to be a way to bring them together," you say to Ted imploringly.

There is something you can do—wait.

Thinking that "it was time" was your first miscalculation! Time for what? And on whose timetable?!

Certainly it is understandable that because you and Ted believe you are going to stay together the idea of one big happy family is simply wonderful. It almost (not quite) wipes out all of those years of longing for an intact family unit. Bliss is just within your reach . . . and you want to grab it.

Unfortunately your children will not want to feel that anyone is being foisted upon them. Their attitudes could easily be something along the lines of, "If you want to go and hook yourself up with someone, fine. But that has nothing to do with me."

In a way they're right.

It is unfair to expect them to create a relationship with Ted's children, or his with yours, simply by virtue of the fact that the two of you are together. As time goes by and they find themselves in each other's company more and more, perhaps over holidays, or other dinners, some sort of uneasy peace will take over, and in a while possibly, a warm friendship.

For now you can't expect them to want to have any rapport. In fact, even if they might have it, chances are they'd fight it.

If you have brought them together prematurely you need to do a little refereeing.

In terms of what you can do right this moment you might want to help the older kids find a tape or CD they can both enjoy together. Suggest, "Look, why don't you guys try and find something you can both enjoy." If they grunt, or look at you scathingly, let it go and allow Lia to sit and read her magazine.

As for the squabbling younger ones, treat it *almost* like a play date. You wouldn't allow that kind of arguing if a friend of your daughter's was over so just do what you would ordinarily. Help them negotiate. "You two have to share. There must be a way to split up the materials fairly." Then sit down and help them out. This is not the extra mile you might go for a play date, but then there are undercurrents in this situation that require a bit more patience and understanding. You know this, even though these young children probably don't.

The one thing you do not want to do is admonish either sets of kids on the grounds that they have to get along. "Listen, you kids are going to be spending a lot of time together so clean up your act" will never do. Nor will "Come on. Please try and get along. Your father and I like each other so much." After all, what do they care? In fact they may even hate that fact! Besides, it really isn't their job to create that big happy family you're longing for. It's something that can happen, but if it does it will develop over time, as everyone builds a history together.

When Ted and his daughters have gone home, it might be a good idea to sit your children down and have a talk about the evening. You'll want to let them air their thoughts, but you may also want to lay down just a few boundaries of your own. While you must certainly allow for your children's conflicted feelings, rudeness ought to be vanquished as quickly as possible.

"Well, that didn't go super well, did it?" you might say, recognizing it's always good to get things out in the open. "What do you think?"

The kids, as you could have anticipated, shrug.

"I don't expect either of you to pal around with Ted's kids, but you know they are company, we don't do this often, Ted means a lot to me, and it would be nice if you tried to cut each other a little slack." You keep it minimal. No major expectations.

"Well, Sandra didn't cut me any slack," Marissa snaps.

"No, it appears she didn't," you agree. "Hopefully Ted is talking to her about that."

"I don't like girls," Joe snaps.

You know he likes them plenty. He's just extremely uncomfortable around them. This is, you realize, an additional reason for him putting on a tape he knew Lia wouldn't watch.

"Well, try not to look at her as a girl then," you say lightly but not without empathy in your voice. "Look at her as Ted's daughter."

You can then sum up the situation with as little emotion as possible in your voice.

"Look, you know Ted is in my life now. And I want him there. He's got kids. We're going to be together sometimes. Just be cool about it. Okay?"

Not surprisingly both of your children nod.

You're clearly not reaching for too much. A little civility. That's all.

Of course, you just can't help yourself. "You may find out you like each other!" you add gaily.

"No way!" both kids ring out, almost laughing as they do.

"Yes, of course you're right," you nod with mock seriousness. Humor, you can see, is going to be a good way to get through this . . . as it is with most difficult situations.

WHEN a parent moves into a serious, long-lasting relationship, children have major issues around change. They are surmountable but you will need to be patient. Naturally you will be concerned that your children like the person you've selected and that he or she likes them. Every tense moment might leave you wishing you could just dig a hole and hide forever—unsure of with whom; him or your kids! You've finally found someone with whom you would like to commit, but it's not just a story about two people. Your children are major characters in this unfolding tale and they will, ultimately, need both of you (in different ways) to happily move forward.

6

Making a Commitment: What Will Make This One Last?

THE time has come for the two of you to say, "We want to share our lives." You may decide to live together, or get married, or live together to see if the desire to marry grows strong. Whichever situation you find yourself in, you are thrilled to have found a soul mate, relieved that the decision of where this relationship is going is over, and looking forward to the grand (though tricky) adventure ahead.

As usual you have your children to think about. They might be excited, not really grasping the changes that lie ahead. They may feel badly, realizing it is over with your ex and wondering what he will think. They may be worried, quite correctly anticipating the unknown changes that will soon occur. And they might be horrified, unwilling to once again alter their world with another change in which they have no say. The announcement that a new person is joining the household may in fact trigger all the old emotions that were experienced first time around when another person *left* the household.

Certainly you will want to create an environment that allows your chldren, no matter what their ages, to air their concerns, hopes, and fears. You will want to proceed slowly, giving your children a chance to first get used to the idea before anything actually happens, and then carefully ease your companion into permanent status in the home all of you (including sometimes his kids) will share.

If you are considering living together, you will want to think about how this is likely to be viewed by your children and those people who are in their world. People *will* have opinions. We've come a long way in terms of our view of what constitutes an authentic relationship, but depending on where you live and the philosophies of family, friends, and acquantances, your unmarried status may be received in a variety of ways.

Unmarried and Living Together

Living together or married there are nitty-gritty details of two adults and families coming together. Understanding the dynamics in the house will help you concentrate on and protect your new, loving, intimate, and sexual relationship.

As the house is rearranged for the arrival of a new permanent figure, it is probable that your child will ask, "Why are you living together and not getting married?" This question may originate in her own mind, or be one that a friend has put to her. No matter what the source of this question, it's an important one to answer.

You are probably quite clear about the complex reasons for your chosen arrangement. Oftentimes, a divorced partner is only a breath away from remembering with piercing anger or hurt the struggle with the legal system, not to mention a spouse, in an effort to dismantle a marriage. "Never again," she might have said to herself. "I can't go through this another time. I don't ever want to talk to another lawyer." Some couples simply opt to live together without bringing the formality of church and state into their union even when they are deeply committed to the new partnership.

Children, however, with their limited life experience, won't necessarily understand the differences, even if they did bear witness to a strife-filled divorce proceeding. You will want to explain that the bond between you and your partner is based on an inner feeling of rightness between you. Papers with signatures are not necessary to prove you want to be together.

Your very little one may be puzzled. "But then he's not another Dad?" or "Isn't he marrying us?" You will want to stand firm and positive. "He loves us but we are not going through the courts," you could say.

You could also reiterate that love is the centerpiece for making a home with someone and your desire and intention to be a good partner and a good parent are very important to you. Go on to explain that your feelings about marriage are not shared by everyone. No one is right or wrong as long as they do what feels good for them. How you and your partner ritualize the partnership is a sophisticated concept for children to grapple with. Learning about what love is and what it looks like in day-to-day terms; caring, sharing, considering each other's feelings seriously; enjoying one another; and hanging in through thick and thin is really what a good human bond is all about with or without a sealed paper. Children with their romantic concept of a marriage might be looking for a celebration "event" to make it real. Something that says, "This is wonderful." If this is the case, you could consider a celebration and special toast that commemorates stepping over this new threshold in your lives.

While this may satisfy your children, if you live in a community in which these values will be challenged, it's quite possible that your kids will be teased and embarrassed by a gossipy buzz emanating from your neighbors, their friends' parents, and even your ex. In this case you might say, "There are some people who believe a legal ceremony is necessary to confirm what they feel inside and others like me who do not believe it makes the love any better." You can also tell your children that when they are older, they can choose to make their partnership official in any setting they so desire.

Avoid telling them (even if you are thinking it) that you want to live together first to see if this relationship really works. Don't color the atmosphere with doubt. If your children know, they may approach the relationship with a tentative commitment. There's no need for an underlying insecurity to be introduced into this arrangement. You've come this far because you feel the real promise. Let the relationship have every chance to flourish.

Once you've handled the basic question, however, you are still going to have to carefully plan the ways in which to help your respective families join each other. This change can evolve into a giant morass of confusion, resentment, fragile acceptance, and fury, making it impossible to understand what is going on and who needs what. Certainly at the beginning it is essential to recognize and understand one of the strongest dynamics that is bound to surface during the transition from a one-adult to two-adult family.

Power Plays: The Search to Know Where I Stand Now

Why do children vie for power? They seek power basically because they have a small amount of it. This decision to bring another adult into the home they share with you was your decision, not theirs. Kids are forever being carted around and told what to do and when to do it. Even if the words "You'll do it because I say so" have never escaped your lips, most parents have had politically incorrect feelings that are tantamount to this stance. Sure, you've made an effort to give your children their say, but in the end kids see themselves as being under your control, and let's face it, for the most part they are. Sometimes this is reassuring for them. A child who knows that he can rely on an adult to be there in predictable ways will feel a sense of safety. But, especially during this time of upheaval, it is critical to strike a healthy balance between being in charge and being overcontrolling. So many big things are happening that involve a complex combination of emotions. If a child is given very little voice in these events, he can feel helpless, angry, and powerless. If a child feels powerless and has little faith in being genuinely considered, a parent leaves himself wide open for power struggles . . . because most children won't give up without a fight.

"Oh Yeah? Make Me!"

The inevitable has happened; Jay has moved in. At the end of the day when everyone converges at home, he is there. At dinner, breakfast, and on weekends when the kids are there, he is there too. The kids try to figure out how to handle this new situation by finding ways to test it. It used to be that when there were family dinners, the focus was on them. This hour over a meal, at the end of the day, was your time to find out what was going on in their worlds. Lively conversations full of questions and responses (and of course monosyllabic answers too) characterized dinnertime in a predictable, comfortable, and loving way.

Certainly, even with a partner, you may try to hold on to this tradition, but the kids watch your behavior closely and are not sure you are as interested in them as you were before. When Jay says something, you quickly turn to him and concentrate on his words. Sometimes you forget to say, "excuse me," when talking to your child, but turn in a split second to the sound of Jay's voice. They may take some action to draw back your attention. They might spill food to create a distraction that forces you to concentrate on them—even if all they receive is your anger. Maybe they'll find an opening to take your side against Jay, thereby making it their camp versus his. Children can become oppositional deliberately. The new guy is wrong, and they are right. They try to get you on their side of the argument and you almost join in, but then something occurs to you. What's the argument? It's near impossible to discern. Yes, tension has been created, or rather manufactured, so that your children can have the experience of all of you ganging up against him. They want him out. They want the power back just the way it used to be. They may fear that if they are too malleable they will lose their important place in the family. A power play is a way to hold on to that place, irritating as it may be.

Your best approach to power plays is to try to calm the underlying fear. If kids fear losing power, help them to feel powerful. Let them lead dinner conversation some of the time or choose the day's activity. Give them a say in what to eat for dinner, what color to paint their rooms, or what video to rent. Wherever you can find a place to put them in charge and give them power over decisions in an appropriate way, let them take the lead. Honor and praise them for their contributions.

Of course, a parent's job is pretty formidable and requires a great deal of patience especially when they are being tested. What can you as the adult do to tolerate being pressured and pushed by a child's psychological demands? It is critical for the adult to stay the adult. You need to develop a way to not personalize what your kid is acting out. Children don't always have the words to explain or the understanding to consider why they do what they do. An adult must stay steps ahead of them, watching, listening, and decoding what a child is really trying to tell you. "I hate spaghetti," your child says, slamming his fork on the table. You might want to say, "Don't bang your utensils," or "What are you talking about? You love spaghetti." But before you do react in this fashion you might want to think about what your child is really saying. "I don't like the way you are treating me, or feeding me. I need more attention and to feel included. I really like spaghetti but not tonight and I want to know if that matters to you enough to give me what I want." A parent can get stuck on the power play behaviors and lose focus on what is really at the heart of the communication. The best way to handle these moments is to look beyond the behavior and get a real feel for what the child is feeling beneath the surface. It does not mean that you have to grant every request; but the mere act of valuing your child's thoughts will be soothing to him. So will naming his fears, sympathizing, and helping him to accept what is appropriate. In this case, a parent might say, "I know you are upset that I didn't give you enough of my time today." And then follow it up with an opportunity to influence the next family decision. The message will be clear. You honor your children's concerns. The spaghetti will likely get eaten.

Kids Have Their Say but Draw the Line Where You Must

Because "acting out" is an indirect behavioral expression of difficult feelings, encouraging forthright statements from your child can cut the confusion time in half. Being open to their saying, "Hey, I don't like this," or, "I have something to tell you," would be very helpful in your quest to keep things running smoothly. It will give you a heads up and a chance to explore the real problem, instead of wasting time on the behavior. "What do you have to tell me?" you might ask in an even tone. Then listen. Let your children have their say but keep in mind that this does not have to mean they automatically get their way. One of the critical ingredients in any relationship, whether it be personal or professional, is the acknowledgment of another person's point of view. This may lead to empathy, sympathy, compromise, a veto, or an agreement to disagree but it's *always* an opportunity to communicate honestly. No one feels ignored. Perhaps you like your house to be super neat, but you can tolerate your child's room being messy if it gives him a sense of power over "his domain." Perhaps if the weekend activity is not your child's first (or second) choice you can offer to invite her friend along so at least she has special companionship. Flexibility will keep your children connected and cooperating with the family, and reduce indirect, acting-out communications.

What? Make Room for Who?

The adult boundaries that hold true for a single-parent household are also applicable in a blended household. As a single parent, you are entitled to personal conversations and interactions with friends and relatives in which your children are not and should not be included. Of course there were probably many times when the boundary slipped and your child played at the foot of your bed as you discussed last night's date with a pal, or your young teen sat outside the kitchen while you listened to a friend expound on the miseries of her lonely life. But now with the new adult in your home, these kinds of lapses will decrease quickly. Your child used to knock on your bedroom door and open it in two seconds; this is no longer allowed. He now has to wait for admittance. And he may find that he is getting many more "just a minute's" before an okay is issued. This may raise his curiosity level and leave him wondering, "exactly what is going on here that I am not part of?" You may find that when your partner is home, you often have to stop your kids from interrupting. There may be more delays before you can sit down and hear them out. The changes may be subtle but they add up and if you are alert you may see your children reacting. All of these changes need to be named, acknowledged, and explained.

Your children are also accustomed to certain jobs and routines. At dinnertime for the last year they made the salad but now your partner feels he would like to put his own stamp on the meal. Well, that was great while you were dating him and he whipped up a nicoise. But now his way is not your kid's way, especially if this isn't a onetime deal. When he starts telling your children to cut the tomatoes in wedges and not slices, you feel a border war brewing. Somehow, this new group will have to find a way to collaborate, cooperate, and integrate new elements. Remember there has to be something in it for everybody to inspire mutual accommodation.

While it's not a good idea for "the new guy" to take over with criticisms and new spins on old jobs, he may instead offer an entirely new recipe to everyone that is free of history or habit. He can be the ringleader in its preparation and take that opportunity to suggest a new way to cut tomatoes "for this dish" or an unusual season for the sauce. In this way he's not changing tradition, but rather adding to it.

If you and your partner make it fun and worth everyone's while the children are likely to play along. (He may still have to withstand some sneers, eye rolling, and jarring comments, however.)

Change rarely goes off without some glitches even when it appears there's everything to gain and nothing to lose.

From your children's perspective even the new recipe, while not interfering with beloved family rituals, may still point to the fact that things are not the same.

Joint Decisions

A new person has different opinions and sensitivities. You never mind how loud your kids play music; he's sensitive to noise. Your kids are not into health foods, but Carol is health-conscious and tends to shop with fat grams and sugars in mind. There hasn't been a container of Heath Bar Crunch in the freezer for weeks. How do you create an environment that is friendly to everyone? That's a good question and one that you might pose to all members of the household together. Brainstorming en masse particularly for kids five and up can be very constructive and feel quite democratic. (Maybe you need to hit the grocery store with your children's list in hand a bit more often!)

In fact, it's advisable during the transition stage to have family meetings devoted to discussing complaints and concerns. This will give the kids an effective say over their home life and keep all family members on top of their feelings. Implement a change for a week and see how it goes, then review it together. Let democracy reign whenever and wherever possible. Sometimes your opinion will have to supercede a child's plan. Everyone knows this. Still, your attitude and the way you bring about and implement change can either set the tone for harmony or give birth to ill will. Playing favorites from the get-go, overriding feelings that should be acknowledged, and generally being insensitive or hurtful will lay the groundwork for unrest that could haunt you for years to come. Quite simply, try to be fair.

Wait Till My New Partner Gets Home

Your new partner may want to be the good guy who is always pleasing and joking or the strong authority figure who lays down clear rules from day one. You may find yourself allowing his more aggressive approach because maybe it's a relief. It's not a job you've ever found so appealing and it lets you off the hook. Of course you run the risk here of making him "the bad guy," which is never a good idea. Or, he may try to create a bond with your kids by being in "cohoots" with them. Rather than discussing allowances, he slips your daughter some cash and whispers, "Don't tell your mother." This behavior creates a false sense of equality, puts one over on Mom and forms what might appear to be a cute alliance. Only in short order he may discover he's created quite an internal conflict for this child who guiltily keeps the money because it's nice to have extra . . . even though Mom wouldn't approve.

The homes that run the healthiest are the ones in which the partners present a united front. Expectations are worked out first between you, then presented to the kids for fine-tuning. Children have a sense of where the adults stand on money issues, chores, sharing, and the general values of the household. Blaming each other or making your part in the equation hazy is a surefire way to add emotional confusion to an already complex atmosphere. Stay away from "I would but he doesn't think we should" or "I'd like to but your mother prefers not to." Adults need to get on the same page, find a place to compromise, and then offer the outcome to your kids while leaving room for them to have some say. It's cleaner and decreases the possibility of them trying to play one of you off the other.

Consider, for example, privacy issues that will likely take center stage once the two of you are under the same roof. Knocking, which may have become a forgotten nicety in your household, needs to be reinstated—but "gently."

"We would like you to knock" is so much straighter than "I don't care but it's important to him." They might, at first impact, like the latter option better because you are siding with their feel-ings, but what will this do for the long-term success of your part-nership and home? If you use the tactic, it's him, not me, don't act so surprised if you overhear, "My mom's cool but it's such a drag since he moved in."

Mi Casa Es No Su Casa

In this new life, children often feel that you are in a huddle with an intruder. There you are talking in hushed tones, keeping them on the outside. Some of these overheard snippets of conversation and some of these new behaviors will come back to you via your ex. Often when a child feels left out, this moves him to tell your ex, "things feel strange at home." Suddenly you feel tattled on. There is a spy among you and it's your own child!

When your ex comes to you with information like, "He says you are forcing him to go hiking," or "The two of you refuse to buy him sneakers," try not to fly off the handle with him or your kid. Your child may be trying to form a stronger alliance with your ex because he feels alone and shut out by your new arrangement, or he is testing boundaries, or he wants to bring the excluded part-ner back into the fold (or fray). Instead, encourage your child to come to you directly with these complaints and explain that the problems that exist in "this family" need to be figured out in this family. Then too, be sure you make the following distinction. You are not asking your child to keep secrets from the other parent but rather to respect that some issues that come up in your household are private and need to stay in your household because it's the best and only place to find solutions. To make this point clearly, you might say, "Remember when you had a fight with Jill? It didn't help to complain to Tammy, did it? Only the talk with Jill did the trick."

If your child overhears intimate conversations between you and your new live-in companion, you may certainly ask that he not repeat the content casually to others. Again, this is a question of privacy. They would not want you to repeat their intimate feelings to anyone and you would like the same respect. It's not that anyone is doing or saying anything wrong when they feel a certain way. It's just that it's information that should be held within the family. You can also make the point that if what they've overheard is curious or troublesome for them you will be happy to try to answer their questions or address their concerns.

I'll Be the Good One

When a family is in the midst of change, each family member vies for a role. Having a place that is theirs assures them an important part of the new family. Even if it's not a positive role it will certainly gain attention.

Sometimes the family makes the assignment for a child or a parent because it's easier than facing a complex problem. Being the scapegoat is common in groups. Here one child is blamed for just about anything: using all the milk and not telling anyone or setting everyone on edge because he never does his chores. Whatever happens in the family always comes down to the fact that he's impossible. This often keeps the family from facing any real problems. Perhaps the two adults in this new household are failing to confront key differences in childrearing. The child, sensing this tension and fearing it, unconsciously decides to be the red herring, and the adults let him because it's easier than facing the true issue. There can also be roles like the brain, the artist, the star and the geek. In a misguided attempt to make one child feel special, parents often unknowingly or sometimes knowingly reinforce roles: "Jenny's the artist here, let her do it; hers will be great." However, this singling out will usually be at the expense of the others. It can be hard work to give every child a firm sense of importance in a family, but characterizing each child one thing or another is an easy out. It only serves to draw walls between the children and leave them wondering what will happen if they fail at what is supposed to be their specialty.

Sometimes there is a goody-goody who wants to be appreciated by everyone and steers clear of conflicts. She can be a welcome but illusory relief to the family. It may seem that at least one person is adapting well, but she may be the one in the most trouble.

Role-playing can offer a safe (if sometimes unpleasant) place to retreat. But it also keeps family members from encouraging each other to be simply who they are.

Hey, This Is My Room

In arranging a new home there are practical considerations over each individual's personal space. It may be part-time or full-time sharing but either way feathers are bound to be ruffled. The kids may want everything to stay the same, but in some areas (literally and figuratively) they may have to compromise. On the practical side, it will help to get the kids involved in setting up the space. Do they need more shelves? Would they like to choose different colors? A room divider? Does anyone need earphones so that one child can play music when the other one is asleep? Try to make the project of converting this space for one into space for two a challenge to their ingenuity. They can't undo the change that is happening but they can participate in many aspects of the form it will take. Convey the sentiment that you need their help. If they accept your challenge, this gives them some stake in making the whole transition work out. Younger kids have a lot to gain in being "roomies" in that the companionship at night can feel like a sleepover date. Some grade-school children who have good chemistry will throw themselves into the togetherness thing. You can offer incentives like bunk beds, which your daughter tells you she "has been waiting for her whole life." Sharing will be experienced with all kinds of imagined and real joys. (You will have to be very understanding when reality sets in.)

One thirteen-year-old girl with only an older brother exclaimed, "I've always wanted a little sister, she's so cute." So far so good. However, bear in mind that teens will likely need and want more privacy than younger kids and if at all possible should have it.

The battle cry "This is my room" is often a metaphor for kids who want to be regarded with respect. They will want to know that you value their needs and that their feelings (and privacy) will be considered and protected by the people they love and would like to trust.

You Offer Encouragement, Then It's Up to Them

Issues of sharing material possessions will often come into question. For younger children, it's okay to guide them toward togetherness. Here, there's still a big learning curve about how to get along with peers and siblings. With older kids, you can offer incentives that will turn into good bonding experiences: hikes, sports activities, and projects that they can complete together and perhaps even get paid for. It's fine to gently provide ways in which bonding can grow but you can't force a relationship. Share your hope and vision in simple ways: "I'm very happy you had a good time," "It's been great that the two of you helped me," "I want us to get along and be there for one another," or "Tell me what would help you be more comfortable together?" But stay away from anything too demanding or insistent, as that will likely backfire.

Your fourteen-year-old son is going to the movies and your new spouse's fifteen-year-old daughter has nothing to do. You think that they should go together and want to suggest it. "Sherrie doesn't have plans tonight." You get a dagger stare. He's embarrassed and angry. "Mom, this is my plan, okay? Sorry, Sherrie, but I'm just going with my guy friends." "It's fine." She smiles weakly. "No problem, I have a report due anyway." Your son has a right to his separate life and so does your partner's daughter.

You've had plenty of time to process this change. En route to this life change, you talked with friends, your partner, read, and contemplated this decision. It is unrealistic to believe that your kids need less of a process. Let them grow into whatever can be real for them.

The "Bicker-sons"

His son is nine, and her son is nine. The fantasy plan was that the boys would share a room and be the closest of friends. The reality is that they draw a chalk line on the rug and forbid the other to walk over it. They fight about everything from tyrannosaurus rex to who played left outfield for the Yankees in 1994. This gives a three-dimensional meaning to "they can't get along, they are so much alike." Sometimes, it feels like the best solution is to close the door to their room for the next ten years and whoever makes it out alive, wins.

These kids are intensely competitive and your new marriage has brought them and their combativeness face-to-face. They are going to have to acquire skills to get along. This move that has altered the uniqueness of their positions (now there are two nine-year-old boys) may in their minds set the stage for wondering "which one of us is better?" Given their druthers each would be the only nine-year-old boy in the house, but since that's impossible someone's got to beat the other to the top. Given their natures and level of emotional insecurity, they may be volleying and vying for first place all the time. You will want to help them get solid and confident internally. This is an opportunity for them to get off the constant external measurement of "I'm better than him" or "I'm not as good as him." More than likely they look at their friendships with others in the same way, which isn't the best for them either.

Help the children in your home feel more secure and competent. Give each child places to shine and stand out. Reinforce that they each have strengths to contribute to the family. Assure them their places are secure in your hearts. In the midst of their fighting for supremacy, take every opportunity to be supportive to both. "Billy, your reasoning is very sound. You do think clearly. But Sam has other ideas worth listening to and considering." Help each of them see they are different but equal in your home.

What starts out as day-to-day bickering could become the catalyst for each to discover a sense of self-worth and confidence. When you help them slow down and take a good look at what is really going on in these fights, they will have an opportunity to realize each other's strengths and will be less interested in pointing out the weaknesses with which each of them might feel afflicted. If a child can learn that he is truly enough, he can stop looking outside himself to see if he measures up. This process will take a lot of time and clarity on your part. It requires an airing of grievances on a regular basis and a walk-through of solutions with careful regard for each kid's self-esteem. Initially this might require physical separations and time-outs. The bottom line is these children have to get along with some civility. There are wonderful life lessons to be had here. All this early training in negotiation and conflict resolution will give them a chance to figure out their worlds in a constructive way.

Romeo and Juliet

Two families are existing in the same space and there are two teenagers—a boy and a girl—who are part of this mix. Both are attractive and know each other from school. All of a sudden, two nice, sexually preoccupied high school kids are living under the same roof part of each week. Hormones are bouncing off the wall. Could this lead to something?

Probably yes. If you leave two attractive, sexually available people alone, the possibility will flutter through their minds that they could get together romantically. After all, their parents sure did. That is not to say that they will act on any of their feelings, and here a parent's preemptive intervention would be a good idea.

Though they are not brother and sister technically by blood, they are now in a home and part of a blended family. This calls for proper boundaries around romantic/sexual contact. First assess through conversation how things are going from each teen's point of view. Ask questions like, "Is it weird to have such a cute guy/girl in the next bedroom?" If you sense an interest, gently underline that it would be a bad idea to put any romantic energy into the relationship and explain how much it could confuse the dynamics in the household. What if one of them gets hurt? Or both? How can they live together under the same roof? All members of the house-

hold will benefit mightily from close sibling-like and parental relationships. Inserting another kind of interest and attraction in the
home could bring tremendous unnecessary and unfortunate tension. You are now all part of the same family and that calls for
lines that are clear and separate.

To further underline your feelings it might be a good idea to
gently enforce a strict dress code even when just "hanging
around" the house. (You'll have to follow it yourself.) Also making
sure each teen invites friends over to introduce their new "sort of"
sibling ("stepsibling" if you're married) will further generate a
safer atmosphere.

The Marriage Crisis

Most people, regardless of their level of emotional sophistication,
come to a second marriage with all manner of fantasies. They may
think their children will feel more secure, or problems with their
ex will ease, or they themselves will finally find the peace they
have been seeking. Sometimes, a vow of permanence does
increase the actual commitment and give everyone a greater sense
of belonging. Partners who become stepparents can assume a
greater sense of responsibility and deepen their bonds with
stepchildren once pledges have been formalized. Marriage can
definitely provide the sense of a strong base.

Children will not usually approach their parent's marriage with
ease and pleasure, even if they really like their new stepparent.
They still are fearful of trusting. One marriage fell apart and this
one could too. They've experienced the loss of their original family unit. How much faith can they have? Then again there are
some children for whom this final step will arouse conflicts of loyalty and betrayal. How, they may worry, will their other parent feel
now that you've found someone and he (she) is still alone? It's
safe to say remarriage is a charged event for everyone. The stakes
are much higher now for parents as they fervently hope this marriage will be a triumph.

"Sorry, But I'm Not Going to the Wedding"

A new marriage can arouse so many charged feelings in a child that his first, second, and third impulse may be simply to get away from it all.

Rule number one. Never force a child who is kicking and screaming to participate in your wedding. Your approach can be gently coaxing, cleverly enticing, or quite direct. But don't push. Suggest finding beautiful dresses and giving the girls a prominent place in the ceremony. Discuss which boys might like to "usher." Younger children may get intrigued with the fun of the plans and not place much weight on what a marriage means to the overall picture. Remember, they are more in the moment, concrete thinkers and thus, often more pliable. "I'm having a good time and so I wanna stay." Older children may be more likely to sense the profundity of what is taking place. Even with all the right emotional support, it is still possible that an internal pressure will keep a child from being able to participate. Often these conflicts can give way to wild inconsistencies. One ambivalent eleven-year-old feared disloyalty to her father and was insistent about not attending her mother's marriage. Interestingly, she was helpful to her mother in finding a dress and accessories. She even said, "I want you to save your wedding dress for me."

Given the discord of her parent's marriage, the new couple, though saddened by her decision, allowed her to be a part of their wedding behind the scenes in any way she could tolerate. They saved her wedding cake and flowers and included her in arranging the photo album.

Everyone Has Wedding Day Jitters

For some couples, planning the wedding and honeymoon for the second time can be as or more nerve-wracking than the first. Running from work to the caterers for food tasting and then sprinting home to cook dinner can be overwhelming. The potentially exciting arrangements, this time around, are taking place within the context of a much more complicated life. And as much as you may understand on an intellectual level the many conflicts that are churned up, you still want a good and beautiful day for you and your partner. After all, haven't you been through enough? you might think. Can't everyone be happy and smile for the camera?

But your children will likely have a growing case of wedding bell nerves as well. As you move nearer to "I do," they may move farther from "My dad's coming back" and fast-forward to "What are we all getting into?"

"Is Your Getting Married Going to Make Things Different?"

Children may carry all sorts of notions about how they think they are supposed to behave now that you are married. They need guidance and reassurance that there is no pressure from you to force a feeling of warmth and love. No, you might say straightforwardly, "You do not have to love him too, but I expect you to be respectful and nice." To lessen their anxiety about the other parent it might be wise for both biological parents to let the child know that they can love, connect, and care for anyone that feels right for them. As hard as it was for one dad to handle his ex-wife's marriage, he took the high road for his son with his wife present. "I love you no matter what or who else you love," he said. "I want you to feel free to be happy and have your true feelings without being concerned that you are doing something against me."

For some older children who have played the part (somewhat inappropriately) of the other adult in the house, the loss of this role can be a blow to their self-esteem. They may experience themselves as being replaced. These feelings can be especially strong if the parent's relationship quickly turned into a marriage, which it sometimes does. ("When it's right," some people believe, "why wait?")

"All of a sudden I don't count?" your thirteen-year-old cried when you had your new wife choose the restaurant for dinner.

Almost every Sunday for three years your daughter has picked the venue. Without any warning (a few times she hadn't been the decision-maker), you pulled this privilege right out from under her. Truthfully, this kind of tangle is highly avoidable. You simply need to think creatively. Perhaps your new mate and your child can take turns choosing the restaurant for Sunday evenings. Gradually, the stepparent and the child might be able to share in certain chores together like planning a menu or doing grocery shopping. The goal here is to make a time for transitions so that a role will not be ripped away from a child and be experienced as an insensitive display of power. Some tangible regard for your child's feelings, and recognition of her "status" as it's been for a few years, needs to be evidenced for her to even begin to accept the new order.

Is There an Adolescent in the House?

By the time most parents remarry, there is often an adolescent in the house. Teenagers can be exhausting for anyone, including themselves. But stepparents can often be on the receiving end of an especially difficult time—even more so than live-in lovers. Now the adolescent has a few "parents" against whom to do battle in their quest for independence. A difficult (or typical) teenager can be hard for any parent to love. Stepparents can often feel pushed beyond their endurance.

One stepmother knocked and entered her stepdaughter's room only to hear the fifteen-year-old scream, "Get out of my room!" Later when she was upset and asked her stepdaughter why she had to behave in that way, the girl replied with complete honesty, "I don't know why I did that, sorry." Her stepmother told her how lousy it made her feel and asked firmly that the girl try to make her desires clear in a way that was less rude and hurtful. She repeated this type of guidance countless times over the years until more civil behavior kicked in.

To cope with the adolescent in your house, read as much as you can about teenage development. Talk to other parents, teachers, watch a couple of teen movies, and know that you are not alone.

Adolescence is a phase that ends when the physiology evens out. Teens are trying to set boundaries for themselves and are so new at it and often so unsure that they go to extremes to make the lines clear. Don't expect predictability. Teens are often struggling with emotions and can go from mood to mood in a matter of seconds. Aim for "respect." Don't ask your teen to be friendly, or smile a lot, or want to hang out with the two of you on a Sunday evening. Require civility. This is a modest request that underlines the fact that everyone counts in the family, but also says to your teen, "I'm not trying to tell you how to feel, but everyone in this house is a person, and I expect you to behave with that simple fact in mind." Illustrate this point by openly and consistently treating your teen and your new mate with respect. Ask for their advice and opinions, listen and be encouraging when appropriate. This is a not-so-subtle way of keeping "the bar" in your house raised to an acceptable level. It's amazing how quickly a sullen teen, left to his own devices, can turn everyone in the house into half-crazed maniacs. If a teen is uncommunicative, try to find activities that you can enjoy together. You may be regularly turned down, but keep asking. Your teen may not look it, but secretly he or she will be glad you're not giving up.

Perseverence pays off. As these tumultuous years come to a close you may just discover that your fortitude helped to create a young adult with a firm sense of self, a great deal of confidence, and a real sense of appreciation for your devotion.

Keeping the Relationship Safe

The crisscrossing of demands from children (and adults) are a major stress on any relationship. They can be particularly hard on the adult who has less of a stake in that child. Many stepparents do not have a reservoir of good experiences to dip into during trying times.

Children may insinuate themselves into your arguments and take sides. Their normal demands may increase in order to keep you closely tied to them, and they may feel more touchy and easily slighted because they "are just waiting" to be pushed aside for the "chosen one."

The truth is, even when the tough times roll and kids have their most fierce reactions to a new marriage, most of them really do not want to ruin things. What they seek is a sense of belonging and reassurances that they have not been replaced. Given a way to connect safely, most kids will accept the marriage eventually. But the early stages can be extraordinarily taxing on your relationship.

What the Adults Can Do for Each Other

Ask for a Partnership. As the stepparent it would be easy to turn to your partner and imply what a miserable job of parenting he or she has done as evidenced by this unbelievably rude child. But if you can muster the restraint, try to say something like, "I don't like it when Wendy speaks to me this way, but I understand it's that she's confused and upset. I'd appreciate it though if you could back me up and help find a way to stop this kind of destructive behavior." It's important then to talk to a child together as a couple.

Remind Each Other This Is a Not-So-Grand Test. Helping each other keep in mind that these impossible behaviors are symptoms and not indications that either of you are living with a "bad seed" will be very helpful. In a way you can become a team of detectives. A child reveals what he feels in the only way he knows how. You are his translator. Your child may be testing to see if you will stick up for him no matter what. How much will either of you put up with before you throw in the towel? Can he trust you or not? Can he take over and squash you like a bug? Working together to "get" what's really happening will underline your commitment to each other.

Present a United Front. As a couple, it is critical to stand together. When you stand apart, do it with dignity and respect for one another's position. Do not break down and take sides against each other in front of your children. You must establish a standard of support within your couple. The boundary must become clear to children. And don't be afraid to say so in words. "You cannot treat either one of us in this fashion. *We* simply won't allow it. If you have a complaint we will listen." The use of the words "we" and "us" will communicate to your child that you intend to stand by each other and that he simply doesn't have the power to rip you apart. This will actually be of some comfort to your child though he may not let you know this is so. He may not even consciously be aware of it. The fact that he can't break the two of you up may free him to find pleasure in your unity.

Finally, here are few more tips on keeping your relationship (and ultimately your children) emotionally together:

- Don't feel guilty taking time for yourselves when your kids say, "You never stay home with us," especially when you know you do. It's easy to think, "Oh no! If that's how they feel . . . what can I do?" Instead, whip out a calendar, point out the last time the two of you went out alone, order the kids a pizza, and leave the number of the restaurant where you will be dining alone!

- Don't allow your children to go on and on about your ex in front of their new stepparent. If they have a point to make, let them make it and then try and move the conversation along to other topics. This will help your new mate to see that you are not interested in allowing your children free reign over their conflicts. If they won't stop, then quietly speak to them alone and clearly let them know that constant references to what their father would say or do in similar circumstances is not something their new stepparent always needs to hear.

- When value issues are going to be on the table, map out a united front before you open up discussions. Children, who are torn by what they want and what's right, can be very confused as they internalize a value system. The more the two of you are in disagreement the more confused they will become. The more confused your children become the more difficult their behaviors will be. If the two of you can't reach an agreement about what's important and what isn't, you are bound for a great deal of conflict.

- If you and your new mate discover suddenly that you disagree on an issue, don't battle it out in front of the children. Recognize the differences and model for your children how to handle such occasions. "Honey, I can see we both seem to feel differently about this. Let's talk about it in private and see if we can't come to a new understanding together." Then turn to your children and forthrightly say, "We'll get back to you when we're clearer about what to do." This will not only display your determination to present a united front, but it will also let your children know that while you aren't simply going to bend to their new stepparent's views, you do respect them. They will see you're willing to think about what's right and not just react. They'll feel important, and you and your mate will have yet another chance to be each other's educator and support.

- Don't be ashamed to make it clear when the bedroom door is closed, it's sometimes closed for a reason. Sure, younger children may grow impatient and be a little hurt, and older children may snicker in their rooms. But with that closed door you will be communicating more than just the fact that you need private time together. You will be modeling for them the importance and value of alone time in a marriage. You will be saying, "When people are happy together they like to be physically close. It's a great thing and something we want in our lives." What better way to give your children a healthy idea about what intimacy between two people is really about? (However, staying in bed all morning while the six-year-olds battle it out in front of the TV is not a wise idea!)

Your children and stepchildren can actually bring your marriage together, as long as you view the job of parenting as one that can be productively and lovingly handled as a team. This doesn't mean there won't or even shouldn't be a time when a disagreement ends with one of you saying to the other, "Well, look. I don't see it that way. But I'll back you up." In fact you should hope this happens now and then. It's an indication that your children are benefiting from the wisdom of different perspectives and that you and your partner can disagree but still operate on a little faith.

Baby Makes Five

Sooner or later, most couples of childbearing age think about having a baby together. This is particularly likely to happen if one person coming into the marriage doesn't have children. Often, the idea of having a baby is "conceived" for many reasons. Perhaps a couple wants to give a single child a sibling. Also, a baby can be a bridge for all of the already existing children. If everyone is included in planning for the baby's arrival, this may provide children with a positive shared experience.

Then again it might not.

Stepparents need to be sensitive about asking the other children to help with preparing the baby's room, thinking of names, collecting their favorite music and old books to share. At first blush these activities can be nonthreatening, cheerful little "jobs" that offer an invitation to stay connected. In preparing the nursery, kids may chat up a storm. Encourage them to fantasize. Will the baby have red hair? Blue eyes? Like the Smashing Pumpkins or Bach, or both? This will make the birth more real and the children themselves feel more involved.

However, your effort to be open does not mean each child will welcome the chance to jump on the bandwagon. Some children will become uncomfortable as the pregnancy becomes more and more visible. For some teens, the outward signs of their parent's sexuality may cause them to seek distance from the event. And of course for everyone, the pregnant mother is a constant reminder that things are about to change yet again.

You may not be able to guess how your child will react, and in fact he may respond differently month to month. One young child walked around at school with a doll stuffed inside her sweater and said that she was having the baby. She wanted so much to be included in the event that she simply "did it too." Another young child cried and cried and said, "How could you do this to me?" He seemed to grieve until a month after the baby's birth, at which time, he proclaimed, "I was lonely without him." As the parent, you will want to stay in touch with the conflicts your children may experience and be sure to give them the permission they need to express their fears. "I'm excited to see the baby, but what if once it's home I hate it?" "I know babies are cute, but what if it's cuter than me?" "I sort of want a sibling to play with, but not if I have to share anything . . . or you."

Generally, with all these fears you simply need to remind your children that this child is going to be an addition to the family and that all of you are in the same boat together. Who knows what it's *really* going to be like? Then remind your children of how permanent your love is for them and end with something of a cry for unity. "We are going to pull through this baby thing together!"

Of course there is the big question, "Are you going to love this new baby more than me? After all, I'm old, and it'll be brand-new, and both of yours, which I am not, and cute and exciting, which I've already been."

It's important not to deny reality, but focus on the excitement, not the love. "Look, of course when the baby first arrives it is going to be exciting. He or she is a whole new being entering our family! But every baby and every child grows cuter and more interesting as the days go by. Your growth and successes and adorableness will always thrill me, new baby or not."

Children will also have unexpected concerns about how this next change will fit into their lives. One child was perplexed that he and his brother would not share the same last name. Would this mean they were not really brothers? Another little boy living among sisters was ecstatic that the baby was a boy. "I'll take him to Little League practice as soon as he is old enough," he said. He felt he had more ownership rights because of gender.

One concern children will not have in advance but will certainly experience once the baby arrives is the uproar it can cause at home. The baby will demand an extraordinary amount of attention, wake everyone up, make Mom irritable, decrease the time any adult has to listen to the stories and problems of the other children in the house, and generally make the household feel like a poorly oiled baby-tending machine.

The best thing to do, in advance of the baby's arrival, is tell the children the truth, and remind them that it's okay to ask for what they need. "Babies are a huge amount of work for the first few months. Mom and I are probably going to be very overwhelmed and it may seem that we are not paying enough attention to you. If that happens, and you have something important to share, speak up. Do it loudly until we listen! Okay? And if that still doesn't work, you can say, *'That baby is driving me crazy!'* I'm pretty sure that will get our attention!"

Whether you're living together or married new difficult situations relating to permanence, loss, and future worry will permeate the minds of your children. It may take a while for everyone to find their balance and to earnestly believe the family is a unit.

As always, especially as children get older, it is important to include them in the planning of such things as vacations. They may feel what they want really doesn't matter anymore because there are so many more people involved. Be careful about any teen who backs off and essentially says, "Whatever." It could mean "You do what you want and I'll do whatever I want."

February school break is approaching and you have planned a week-long vacation. This is your first time away together since you have become a "family." You found out about a beach house in Mexico that was affordable and your partner thought it was a good idea. The two of you presented it to his daughter and your two daughters as a surprise. Only your fourteen-year-old daughter, Lily, seemed

unenthusiastic, but then she has been slow to come into the family fold. She is a teenager and in a tribe apart these days anyway.

Three days before the departure date, Lily tells you that she has decided not to go. "Don't worry," she offers, "Dad said I don't have to and I can stay with him." You disagree with this entirely, and feel angry at your ex for deciding this without discussing it with you first. The power and authority has been pulled out from under you, and besides that you simply want her to go.

It's a family vacation. You have the ticket, the accommodations, and you have been searching for ways to bring her more firmly into the family unit. She has to go. Of course if you hit her with this head-on you will lock horns, and nothing except angry feelings will come of it. You decide instead to look to see what might make it easier for her to enjoy the idea of coming along.

"Why don't you want to go on this trip?" you ask. You shake your head when she answers, "I don't know, I just don't," and "It doesn't make any difference." You both know it makes a great deal of difference. You would miss her terribly and you are quite sure she would feel abandoned if you just gave in on this one easily. "I love you and I want you to be with me, with us; it's our first time all together," you say matter-of-factly.

"I know," she says, "But I don't want to be all together, I'm sick of all these people. Maybe you can take it but I can't, not for a whole week. I need time to myself. Besides no one even asked me if I wanted to go in the first place. You just expect me to want to because you want to."

"I think I made a mistake planning it as a surprise." You nod in agreement. "Now that you are upset, I realize I should have talked with you about it. Why didn't you tell me instead of going to your father first?" Lily shrugs. "You have Jay. The two of you are always snuggling, and the kids are both ten and have each other, so I'm the odd man out." And there it is.

Lily is basically saying that not only does she feel that she has no power in the situation, she also feels like the odd man out. She feels outnumbered and alone so she leveled the playing field with her father's backing. By discussing the situation you can reach some logical compromises. The two of you would spend some private time together and she was also given permission to explore the possibility of one of her friends joining you for the week.

Lily's power play was rendered unnecessary by outlining some limits and giving her some power. You also called your ex and suggested that in the future, it would be wise not to figure out "solutions" to problems in your home without first informing you of the issues at hand.

His and Her Rules

There will come a time when you will be away and the new stepparent will be in charge. This can be a problem. Yes, she is the adult in charge. Yes, she is the parental figure. But she's certainly not the one your kids are used to and they will not go down without a fight if there is a disagreement on the table.

Your new wife grew up in a home with a lot of rules. This has always been hard for your daughter to adjust to. You have kept a low profile around this tension and all three of you have coasted in a distant, polite way for about a year since your remarriage. Suddenly, all hell breaks loose. You are in a hotel on a business trip and your sixteen-year-old daughter is on the phone, upset because her stepmother is refusing to let her best friend stay over. "Daddy, Kelly's mother is away and I said it was okay, it was always okay before, and it's always okay with Mom. Besides, Donna is not my mother." As a married man and then a single dad, you figured if your kids got their homework done and could get up for school the next day, a weekday sleepover was fine. You never knew that sleepovers could be an issue because it never came up in your old or new marriage until now. Now your wife comes to the phone. "I don't feel it's right during the week." Your wife is holding steady to this position. "Plus she didn't tell me about it until three minutes before she called you." You feel the vice tighten.

You agree with your daughter that it is no big deal. It's been a no-brainer for the two of you; you've always casually allowed sleepovers. If you tell this to your wife, she will feel embarrassed and betrayed in front of your daughter. If you tell your daughter to defer to her stepmother, you will feel wimpy changing the known rules in midstream. It's a rabbit-in-the-headlights moment. You've let too many things slide between them to keep the peace and now you are caught.

At first, you try to squirm out of it, but then feeling awful you step up to the plate, asking both of them to get on the telephone.

"Obviously, we have two different takes on the same situation," you say. "I've always allowed Debbie to have weekday sleepovers and that's what she is used to." "Yeah," Debbie mutters. Then she shouts, "I didn't want this damn family, I can go stay with Mom or Cousin Julie; I don't need this grief. She is on me all the time— I get A's, I tiptoe around her, and I have to do this too. Donna," she repeats, "is not my mother. Besides, you guys sleep together every night. I'd like to have company too!"

For a moment both you and your new wife are stunned into silence. You had been about to launch into a brief speech about Donna certainly not being her mother but the one in charge of Debbie's well-being at the moment.

But suddenly your sex life has been drawn into your teenage daughter's sleepover needs? A moment later it makes perfect sense.

Your new sex life doesn't escape her notice for a minute. Whether or not it's really why she wants a sleepover your daughter has found a way to stick it to you. She's saying, "You think I don't know you used to do it with Mom, and now you and your new wife are at it?"

You may be stunned and not know what to say, but now that everything is out in the open it has to be dealt with. Unfortunately, in this family, so much has been pushed under the rug that it has become explosive. Debbie has been compliant at a time when her teen hormones are pushing for separation and independence. The pressure of being the goody-goody has backfired and so has her apparent notion that you think she doesn't really know what goes on behind closed doors.

The parent's best bet here is to start to get a good dialogue going. You say, "This change has been so dramatic for all of us, I'm so sorry I haven't gotten us talking more. You both sound so hurt." Addressing your daughter, you say, "You're right. I have great company at night and I'm glad of it." This will immediately give your teenager the message that you think she's old enough to deserve the respect of acknowledging her growing sophistication. And to your (likely flattered) wife you say, "Here you are in charge of my daughter, a teen, and it's been so much, too much to expect it to be easy. I feel I've left too much to you and I've been unfair. As for tonight, because it has always been fine with me, would it be all right to go ahead with the sleepover? It's late and as long as the girls are cooperative, would you just allow it?"

Without a lot of attention and genuine care and empathy, many homes fall apart over these issues. Teenagers are already challenged with feeling needy and at the same time having to be independent and more responsible for big decisions like which romance and academic tracks to pursue. A remarriage is another major adjustment. If they have an alternative, many teens will forsake one home for another unless they feel regarded in a loving and fair way.

"I Think You're in the Wrong Place"

Younger children don't understand lust. Slightly older children have some idea of what it means but would rather not know more than what they've already figured out. This doesn't mean they can be allowed to get in the way of it. You will want to keep some spontaneity in your sexual life and on occasion your children and an hour of passion will be at odds.

Your children cannot win every time. Unless it's an emergency you and your new mate would do well to assure each other that your physical intimacy matters and is not about to be tossed away simply because of a seemingly needy child whose needs can be attended to after you've made love.

Your new husband has been away on a business trip all week and it's now Sunday morning. You've both woken up feeling "frisky" and before the two of you get started with some passionate lovemaking he uses the bathroom. You're lying there smiling with your eyes closed when suddenly you feel a slight stirring in the bed beside you that does not sound like your mate. You open your eyes and there's your ten-year-old daughter, snuggling under the covers (as she'd done the other morning) smiling contentedly. You are profoundly glad you happen to be in your nightgown but your husband is about to walk out of the bathroom and you know you have to think fast.

"Honey," you say, pulling the covers off of her, "not now. I haven't seen Glen for a whole week and we want to spend a little time alone this morning."

"But why?" she asks. "Didn't you talk last night?"

"Yes, we did," you say, climbing now out of bed yourself. "But we're not done yet." You take your pouting daughter by the hand and walk her to the door. "Scoot," you say firmly. "I'll talk about this with you later."

Around an hour or so later, bathrobe on, you enter your daughter's room where she is sitting up in bed reading. She looks at you warily, not sure what's coming or if she's going to get yelled at.

"Sweetie, I just want you to know I love you a lot. I know things are different now. You've been climbing into bed with me for years. And sometimes even now, it's okay. But you know what? Since Glen is here I think it would be a good idea for you to just ask first. That way I don't have to send you away and you don't have to feel bad."

"But why couldn't I have just stayed there on your side of the bed with you?" she asks.

"Because it was a time that Glen and I needed to be alone. It's a being married thing and one day you'll understand that completely. That's just the way it is. There are loads of time when you are included!"

Then you immediately follow that statement up with proof.

"Like now! Come help us make waffles."

Of couse what if you have a more sophisticated ten-year-old who you sense knows exactly what's going on. Your approach requires being straight but short on detail.

"Sweetie, I love you but I want some time alone with Glen."

If she says, "I know why," in that snotty little way she has, don't bat an eyelash.

Just smile and say, "I bet you do."

This will not only shut her up, but likely send her running for the hills of her own bedroom as fast as her fluffy pink slippers will allow.

PROTECT your marriage by giving each other as much emotional support as possible. You will likely be in the house with a hive of irritated bees. Respecting everyone's rights is the only way to keep peace in the nest.

7

Widowed and Dating: But Daddy Just Died (A Year Ago)!

THE steps in seeking a romantic life when a partner has passed away are different from those for the divorced parent. When the union is lost through death, both parent and child will probably have a particularly difficult time with feelings of disloyalty, guilt, and grief. The range of response to the loss can be evidenced by the creation of a shrine (perfumes, hairbrushes, shavers, and neckties strewn on bureaus and countertops) or attempts to put every memory away, and everything in between. As in any life change—and death is certainly the most profound and final—the variety of feelings surrounding the event have to be felt and processed, shared and released in order for a family to allow life to move forward.

It is important to understand some basic issues surrounding both your loss of a spouse and a child's loss of a parent because they will impact heavily on a child's ability to allow himself as well as *you* to move on.

A Loss of Balance

After a divorce family members will find there are some changes in relationships because of distance, visitation rules, quickly shifting emotions, and more. Each family member will change in various ways. But when a loved one dies any opportunity for an evolving relationship no longer exists. The absent person lives in memory and essentially does not change.

Because this loss is permanent and (unlike divorce) one that no one wanted, you or your child may be stuck living life on an emotional treadmill. In an effort to stay connected to a spouse or parent with whom no new day-to-day experiences can be had you may revisit past experiences again and again. If you or your child are dwelling on the past how can feel free to reach out for new sources of love? It may feel as if letting go of the past also lets go of the person. Enjoying life may mean a new partner, but in so doing you may feel as if you are leaving your deceased beloved behind, which can feel like an unacceptable betrayal. But it is critical to realize that failing to find a balance between your past and present is the biggest betrayal of all . . . of you and your family. It is important that all family members find the strength to go on and once again experience pleasure.

Making a new life requires a deep sensitivity, awareness, and acceptance of the past. It also requires feeling a connection to it while still finding the strength to form a relationship to the present and future. A parent who is gone can never be forgotten or wiped out of his family's lives. He lives on in particular rituals: certain prayers, holiday meals, in pictures, items once belonging to him that can still be used, in thoughts, and in your heart. But you and your children deserve to have new love in your daily lives. Gradually, thoughts of the deceased parent/partner should be allowed to recede—to take up a smaller part of your lives. This is not an act of disloyalty. That "smaller part" will always be golden, ever present somewhere inside everyone, and when it is needed most it will always be available. Actually, it is a position of honor.

Your child will undoubtedly follow your lead when it comes to what feels acceptable and what does not in the face of a profound loss. No matter what the circumstance of the death, your child's feelings and the way he handles them will be powerfully affected by the way in which you express and deal with your own. Whether you are in denial, guilty, depressed, angry, reflective, or melancholy, it will not go unnoticed. The key to moving past the grief and leaving yourself and your child open to other people, rests with the amount of honesty you can bring to the grieving process, thus giving your child permission to do the same.

In fact, *permission* is key to healthy grieving. Because there's no right or wrong way to grieve, what you and your child do should be respected, and if necessary, attended to. Sometimes people who are grieving together need to face their pain separately as well. Sometimes they need the help of a professional. It can be a good way to let some fresh air into the darkened rooms that exist both literally in the home and figuratively within the hearts of you and your children.

Did You Get to Say Good-bye?

A person's readiness and a child's ability to seek and accept new love depends very much on the relationship with the lost parent. Sudden deaths cause greater trauma. One has no opportunity to prepare for the loss, say good-bye, resolve nagging issues, and/or make some kind of peace. One four-year-old girl whose mother was killed in an auto accident insisted this happened because she had been naughty in refusing to get dressed in the morning. At her age she is operating egocentrically. To her young psyche her bad feelings became empowered with magic that was powerful enough to have caused the tragedy. Self-blame set in fiercely and laced her grief with an unwieldy intensity. Her grief and guilt had to be dealt with by a loving family and counseling. Gradually, over time and with consistent care, she was eased out of her enormous guilt. Finally, she could move through her grief and sense of loss free of other complex and painful thoughts and begin to enjoy loving and supportive memories of her mother.

If a partner is ill and has a condition that leads to a slower passing on, there is time for thoughts and feelings to be shared. Perhaps the ill parent will have the wherewithal to let a child and a spouse hear how much they want them to go on to have a happy life. These words are very helpful in freeing a person to love again. However, it is also possible that someone who is terminally ill will be in a state of denial and have such a hard time with his own condition that he is unable to convey such magnanimous thoughts. A parent's denial will affect a child's ability to reckon with the gravity of a situation. In fact, a child will want to cling to denial as well because the thought of losing a mother or father is so unbearable. In these situations it is best for the other parent to at first gently bring their child around to the realities of at least the illness so that the child is aware this situation is not going to have a happy ending. Then when the parent is very close to death it would be a good idea to inform the child that the parent is going to die. But this must be done carefully. A younger child who is told his mother is going to die too far in advance will find the job of hiding this "secret" from her so unbearable that it could wreak havoc with his own already fragile ability to cope. The resulting internal conflict could be long lasting, further complicating the grieving process. However, as the time draws near, denying a reality that the child can surely sense, will only make him more anxious. The key is for the well parent to encourage discussion with the child about how he perceives things and how he feels. Permission to speak will keep this child on a healthy track.

The Guilt of Resentments

In some families in which a person dies after a lingering illness, there are discomforts and resentments generated by the sick parent's growing unavailability and need for more care and time. It's hard for anyone to feel okay with the anger they might feel toward someone they love who is so sick. The day-to-day grind and demand can wear on the physical and emotional energy of healthy people. For children and adults, the sights and sounds of illness can be frightening and sickening. Secretly, caregivers or even children watching the slow deterioration of a loved one may wish for relief from this awful time. One child said, "I want Mom to live but I hate the coughing, the spitting up, the crying, that she can't skate with me, run with me, read with me, or even show up for my school play." It's not that this child or any other child or adult wants a beloved person to die . . . it's that they want the emotional agony to stop for everyone. But few people give themselves the "permission" to think these thoughts. "How can I wish death would come already?" they might think. "What if it were me? What kind of person am I?" This is what is known as "survivor's guilt." The spouse who is left can wonder why he or she was spared the illness and feel the guilt of knowing life will continue for him or her. This guilt however, left alone, can stand in the way of those who are left behind finding the strength and freedom to love again. After all, with such dreadful thoughts, do you even deserve to have a good time?

While you may no longer be forced to endure those pictures of impending death the dying person will also no longer have to deal with the pain that created them. Yes, he or she has been cheated out of more of life's wonderful experiences—experiences you might in fact have the good fortune to enjoy. But neither you nor your child are to blame. Guilty feelings need to be raised and discussed as openly as is tolerable. As the adult, however, it would be best to keep the intensity of your guilt between you and perhaps a counselor. Remember your child will take his cues from you. Your child's guilt will likely be a bit less laden than yours and will need to be dealt with appropriately. If for instance you are about to go out to the movies with your children, and one says, "Mommy would have loved this. Maybe we shouldn't go," this is a perfect opportunity to give your children permission to keep moving. "Honey, it's true she'd have loved it and it feels terrible that she's not getting a chance to enjoy it with us. But I know she'd want us to go. Remember how happy she would be when anyone of us had a good time whether or not she was with us? Let's try and remember that."

By saying things like this you will be reminding both you and your child of her abiding love, and slowly, gently moving away from thoughts of what could have, or should have, been. Accepting that you have survived and giving yourself permission to continue and take part in the world is a major and necessary accomplishment when someone you love dies. Your kids will look to you, their role model, and they will follow where you are leading. They will internalize the rules given verbally and silently about what they can and can't have for themselves by sensing and knowing what you allow for yourself.

Ready or Not

Each family member grieves at a different pace and in their own style. When one is ready to move beyond the loss, another family member may not be ready. One dad may be ready to date while his six-year-old daughter is still crying every night and snuggling Mommy's favorite pillow. The road to recovery will be smoother if this discrepancy can be respected and addressed.

One little girl heard her father on the phone making a date with a woman for dinner and a movie.

"But Mommy died," she said plaintively as soon as he got off the phone, as if that fact should dictate how they live their lives from this point forward.

It is important to let children know that it is fine for them to be in a different place in their feelings than you are. This little girl needed to stay with memories and feelings of her mom and may want her dad to be exactly where she is too. Your company in sadness is comforting. Suffering alone is not. It is helpful to reach for commonalties. If you empathize and explain that some days you feel the way she does, and that you understand what she is feeling, she will be more accepting of the differences between you. "Everyone's feelings can go up and down like a seesaw" you might say. "Imagine us on side-by-side seesaws. Sometimes we'll be moving up and down together, other times we won't." Of course it is also important for adults to maintain stricter privacy if they believe their activities will really be too hard for their children to handle.

This is true for an older child as well, particularly from about age eight and up. They will more easily grasp the concept of people moving at different paces because they have already begun to see their peers making strides at different rates and in different ways in reading, math, athletics, or music. You can draw parallels here with the pace of grief. To be sure, if you're feeling low but sense your child is looking forward to a social evening try to be encouraging. "I'm so glad you're going out. Have a great time!" Your child may need your permission to let go of his sadness. He's likely to think that if you say it's okay, then it must be, even if he senses you are staying home in the doldrums.

Keep differences in mind when it comes to the ways people comfort themselves as well. The same activity may connect one person too closely to the loss, but provide relief for another. For example, bike riding during the week of a funeral can seem outrageous to one family member, but to the biker, it may bring back lovely memories of a ride with the person they've lost. It may also be a good way to release pent up feelings.

Family members will do better if they are open to and respectful of each other's worries, sadness, guilt, anguish, ambivalence, and relief whether the death is sudden or anticipated. It is crucial not to force or push anyone away from emotions they need to experience. Asking, "How can you say/feel that?" is damaging. People are entitled to how they feel and in fact to express how they feel in whatever way they can. Sometimes their chosen words may inaccurately express how they feel but simply be a product of that person's desire to hide from pain. One adolescent upon learning his mother had finally died, asked, "What are we going to do without her teaching salary?" The real question was, "what are we going to do without Mom," but she couldn't move to that until a week or two later. Some family members might run right out to "have fun" desperately trying to stave off the pain. This behavior can look disloyal when it is simply a misguided attempt to avoid grieving.

Death is traumatic. People of every age need room to grieve and cope in the way that works best for them. Permission to do so paves the road to once again allow for happiness and love for each person in accordance with his own readiness.

Permission to Date

As a parent, you have to be strong for your kids and hold the remaining family together. At a certain point that will include dating. On the one hand, dating can symbolize a positive move forward, and on the other hand, it can be seen by many children as a decrease in the love you feel for their deceased mother or father. It may be difficult for all surviving family members to emotionally understand that having a relationship in the present does not lessen the importance of the parent who has passed away. But in time, as the need for new loving connections grow, most people will come to embrace this truth.

However, everyone moves at a different pace and some people will take quite a while to give themselves permission to date.

Sometimes not pursuing an adult life is a relief. You've been so hurt at the loss of your spouse that the idea of getting out there and dating feels too daunting. It's been years since you flirted, had a physical relationship with a new person, or simply had to present yourself in a style to attract others. In fact, the mere thought of it makes you run for cover. That cover all too often can be your companionable children who, snuggling with you in front of the VCR, are great Saturday night "dates." You can come to rely on them just as much as they rely on you. This can be a danger. Some parents look to their children to meet the social and emotional needs of a partner. The kids become confidants and behave like dates. They hang out and accompany you to weddings and outings, which is not good for the child or for the parent. Though it is overwhelming to begin again, it is important for a widow or widower to eventually seek adult company to meet their adult needs. Kids who have lost a mother or father and who are forced to witness the grief of the surviving parent are often all too willing to seek some new indispensable role in family life. "Protecting" the parent who is left behind is sometimes used as a substitute for grieving. The child's emotional energy is taken up "caring" for their parent. This will not serve either parent or child well. For the experience of loss to proceed in a healthy way, parents and children have to play their appropriate roles as well as have their current needs met.

The first time your child witnesses you hug or kiss another adult will be a milestone in the recovery process. Feelings of anger, confusion, and relief may permeate the air: If your children bring it up, try to give an answer that speaks to the love you had in the past and would like again now. "We all need love and affection in our lives, but I will never forget the way I shared those things with your mother." This is a wonderful way to model how the present doesn't have to desecrate the past.

"I'll Do It for the Kids"

Sometimes jumping quickly into a new relationship can be caused by guilt. A "replacement" parental figure can seem the way to gain some control over the situation and give back to the kids what they have lost. "My kids need a mother," one man replied when asked why he was marrying so soon after his wife's passing. But a quick leap into a new relationship may be used to cover pain, or signal a need to deny the death of the spouse and the loss of what was. There are no shortcuts for mourning. If the family has not grieved properly this new union is bound for trouble.

There are times when parents may be ready to begin dating but cannot face their need head-on. They say, "Well, I'm not ready, but I believe my children need it." If this is the springboard necessary for you to launch into dating so be it. However, it would be far better to accept the readiness for what it is: the very human need for an intimate relationship. This way, when the pleasures of once more experiencing love reappear, you can enjoy them most fully.

"How Can I Leave My Kids, with What They've Just Gone Through?"

Guilt can keep a widow or widower from dating. These parents may believe that their children have sustained such a loss that they must be available to them twenty-four seven. To compensate for their children's loss, they will be both mother and father to them and shield their children from further hurts even if it means sacrificing an adult life. This self-sacrifice can go on for years.

They worry that a remarriage may put their children in financial jeopardy if anything were to happen to them. Or, they stay away from the entire dating arena because they fear loving again. One loss has been enough and they cannot imagine putting themselves or their child through another. After all, there's no guarantee that a new spouse will stay well.

The truth, however, is that children are resilient and it's important for them to see a parent (in spite of the pain they have all endured) take a risk and believe in life and the goodness of new connections. "Leaving" your children for an evening out is a way of bringing them hope. Finding yourself in a new relationship is actually a way to "return" to them a parent who can enjoy and model what it's like to love another person. This is the parent they once knew. When you can form a new relationship, in many ways you are doing the opposite of leaving your child. You are signaling that you are "back."

A Heads Up to Parents

Your child has been hurt. The healthiest thing you can do is acknowledge the pain, loss, and grief, speak of its unfairness, and share in the anger and sadness. You can also encourage them to view life as something that still has to be led with a sense of responsibility to others, facing challenges, and realistically addressing everyday concerns. You can tread lightly and make allowances for emotional outbursts, sudden unrealistic demands, or rudeness if that is how your child vents. But often parents go too far. . . .

- Indulging their children's emotional demands and needs in order to compensate for the loss of a parent.

- Filling the loss with material things and too much sacrifice.

- Role reversals—letting children parent you because you are so grief stricken and needy and it seems to make them feel good.

- Letting kids use guilt to manipulate you into not moving on.

There is a difference between relaxing some rules and allowing for some extravagances to provide a bit of comfort. But keep in mind "a bit" is precisely all you will get. In the end the loss has happened, and piling up new privileges, gifts, or extending an inordinate amount of tolerance for poor behavior will do nothing but create a lack of structure at the precise time that everyone needs it to feel secure and connected.

Children's Reactions to Dating After a Death

In general children idealize the parent who has passed away and as a result no one can ever compare. They have a tendency to remember a model of perfection and with a level of specificity that is simply uncanny.

"That's not the way Mommy makes pancakes." There will be negative comparisons, resistance, and anger toward someone new being in the place of the deceased parent.

"What do we need her for? We are doing okay with just us." A child who has finally found some emotional balance after the death will not want to shake anything up again. He especially won't want to open himself up to a new person. Enough is enough.

"What would Daddy say?" A child, unwilling to completely let go of a deceased parent may still cling to what she perceives would be her dead parent's wishes. This question could easily pop out in front of a date—just to make sure everyone remembers.

After the mourning period has been observed and a parent turns his or her attention to finding connection, solace, and comfort with adults of the opposite sex, children will have a wide range of reactions. Many children verbalize to their parent that it is okay to go ahead and date, some even encourage it, expressing a sincere desire that Mom or Dad no longer be alone.

When dating begins, however, children can be confronted with many feelings that they may not have realized were roiling inside of them.

For very young children, death may not be perceived as permanent and final. The concept that someone is never coming back is incomprehensible. They will ask when Mom or Daddy will be back. Often, they will want to write cards or ask to call them in heaven. One little girl who was told at three that her mom became a star asked at age four, while riding in an airplane, if she could go and make a visit to Mommy since they were so close to her in the clouds. When you begin to date this child will sense the importance of this new person's presence but will likely not be able to place him or her in any real context. It should suffice to simply say, "This is my new friend."

Slightly older children may react to a date with confusion, anger, or even needy desperation. "That's my mom's coffee cup," one five-year-old said with irritation to her father's date. "You can't use it! My mom will be mad." This child knew his mom was gone but on some emotional level had not yet accepted it. Another young child, in an effort to completely deny the loss, practically joined at the hip with the first woman her father dated. She would hop onto her lap and try to get the physical comfort and security she had been used to getting from her mother.

In general, another man or woman on the scene forces children to face the utter hopelessness of their parent ever returning. If that new person comes into their home regularly, it can feel like salt in a wound, disrupting the reruns with Mom or Dad that they play over and over in their head in order to hold on to life as it used to be.

A new adult brings a new sound of laughter; a new opinion intrudes and takes up the empty space. A new person presents similarities and contrasts to what used to be normal. Children will want their mother or father back, "the way it was." But very little will ever be the same after sustaining a death in the family. Normal will simply have to become something else. The letting go of waiting or hoping for everything to be like it was can be a difficult process and for many never fully happen. Children should be helped to understand these feelings are normal—but that while they may still wish for what was, everyone's hearts are big enough to enjoy and love new people. Yearning does not have to be prison.

One teenager who had stoically handled his father's death had his bubble burst when his mother became serious about a new man. Her new relationship called up his intense longing for his father in a way his "absence" had not because he had avoided the finality of death by emotionally viewing his father's "disappearance" as an incomplete story. A person cannot return from death, but an absence is another matter altogether. When his mother began to date, this teenager could no longer deny the death and it was really only then that he began the real process of grieving. It was necessary for this mother to keep much of this new relationship away from her son—not denying it—but not complicating her son's grief with concerns or fears as to how to relate to this new man in her life. She also got her son counseling to help him face the feelings he had avoided for so long.

When it comes to a child's reaction to your dating life after a parent dies, anything can happen. The key is to stay tuned to where your child is in the grieving process so that you do not pressure him to move on, to see life as still opening up before him, before he is ready.

Don't Date in Secret—Just Date Quietly

After one parent has died children can become extremely worried about losing the other both in a physical and emotional way. Initially when a parent is late coming home, or gets caught in a storm, children can become extremely worried. But even when time has passed and you begin dating your children may now be fearful of losing you to another person. Of course this is true in a divorce situation as well, but at least most times there is the other parent to whom they can retreat. When they have lost one parent, they have only you to rely on now. Each child will be able to handle knowledge of your dating life in their own way. Some children will do better at least at first if they do not witness your budding love life at all for a while—though certainly it should not be a secret that you go out.

Unfortunately, keeping dating out of a child's view can be a logistical problem for the widowed parent. One woman who lost her husband at age forty-six waited about a year before accepting an invitation to dinner from a coworker. She hadn't expected a reaction from her child because they had grieved so much for so many months but when this man came to pick her up, her fourteen-year-old daughter became absolutely robotic. She was artificially polite and acted as if ice were running through her veins. As soon as he came into the living room, she greeted him and then disappeared as fast as she could. Later, the girl reported she cried and cried because seeing the new man made her miss her father even more.

"I felt so guilty putting her through more suffering but I was lonely. I'd had a good marriage and I missed the companionship. I wanted to keep dating but I began doing it more on the sly. I even lied sometimes, telling her I was over at Aunt Bonnie's. Now I was like the teenager, lying and keeping secrets." Occasionally, however, she allowed a date to pick her up. Her daughter, she knew, was going to have to get used to it sooner or later.

It's a positive choice to protect and not overstimulate your children by bringing every date into their lives. At the same time, keeping secrets can set their minds racing. They have sustained a major trauma (as have you) and they are vulnerable to fears about the sharp turns life can take. They will feel disoriented for what might be a long time and need reassurance about their importance to you. Their concerns will rest largely on two things. How will they fit into a new configuration, and will you honor Mommy or Daddy's memory? Too many secrets may leave them guessing and will only raise children's anxieties. A balance must be found between protecting your child from knowing too little and fearing too much.

Keepers of the Flame . . . and Trial by Fire

Quite often after a marriage breaks up, the homes of each partner are cleansed of most of the couple memorabilia. This is tolerable because life with Mom or Dad is continuing though in separate places. A child can ask one or the other parent as often as he wishes what it was like when "we" did this or "we" did that. But with a death, the remaining parent and child hold the memories together and must find some way to keep them alive. The past will be present in the home in the form of framed photos, keeping rooms as they were before the death, and speaking about the lost one in conversation.

To an extent maintaining memories is all part of mourning, but it can get out of hand and create an environment that gets in the way of moving into the dating world. Pictures around the house displaying wonderful family moments can and should always be present. However, if after around six months, for example, a hairbrush with the deceased parent's hair still entangled in the bristles rests on the bureau it can be a problem. It can speak to an unwillingness to believe the person is gone. Less intimate items such as coffee cups or favorite needlepoint pillows can hold lovely memories and needn't be "shrine-like" in their visibility. But if you are unable to take your spouse's coat out of the hall closet or her winter hat from the family basket of snow clothes, your children will notice and be forced to face the loss during the most mundane moments. They may lose the joy of building a snowman when they spot their father's gloves.

Each time this happens it will keep them from "letting go" inch by inch so that all of you can move ahead.

There's another problem with little shrines. Not only can they keep you and your children enmeshed in the past, but they can help to create an environment no new lover can possibly enter.

A person who dates a widow rather than someone who is divorced will undoubtedly find him or herself in a difficult situation. Putting aside the comparisons and difficulties with which you may struggle, silently, your children will present a major challenge. They may regularly remind your date of the personality and qualities of the deceased parent. "My mother *always* liked to cook," one young boy announced when his father's date admitted she wasn't exactly a chef. One little girl continually referenced her mother whenever her father brought home a date. It seemed as though the mere sight of another woman set off a flood of memory for her. She clearly felt unsafe being in the present, and thus maintained control of her emotions by repeating experiences with her mom from the past: "We always ate muffins on Sunday" or "My mom let me play my music loud." Even the most patient, understanding dates will feel (if not say) "I am not your mother; I have my own ideas." It will be extraordinarily unpleasant for your date to be reminded that she is always in the shadow of someone else in the eyes of the children (and you).

This is a difficult spot for a parent to be in because it is important for children to be able to express their ambivalence and pain. It can be very upsetting to have to put your children first as your child spins stories about the greatness of his lost mom or dad, when at the same time you can see your date's face sink. But how can you ask a child to talk less? You cannot shut a grieving child down with a look or a glance. You cannot warn them not to speak freely.

On the other hand you can say and do things so that your

child's tendency to go on and on is modulated and/or encouraged for another time. A child who likes to talk about how great his dad was at playing kickball can be told, "It's true, Dad was really quick at that move, but let's just have a good game now with Stan. Maybe later you and I can play another game and you can show me again how Dad used to do it."

It's also important to help your child pay some attention to how he or she can make others feel. "I know you love your mom and that's very important and wonderful but when you make everything she did the best and make what Lynn does feel always bad, it hurts her. No one can replace your mom, and Lynn isn't trying to. But she does have her own special qualities to offer. It would be great if you could try and see what they are."

Because the issue of a parent's death needs to be attended to with a particular understanding, it is very helpful if you and your date/partner can talk over how to deal with a child who is clearly having trouble adjusting to the idea of you having a new romantic partner.

Your new partner might:

- Show interest in the lost parent. Statements like "Oh, you saw that with your mom," or, "Was blue your mom's favorite color?" let a child know that she can accept the former relationship and not be threatened by it.

- Point out any honest similarities between himself and the deceased parent. This may make a child feel a little closer to him. For example, "*The Wizard of Oz* is one of my favorite movies too."

- Be encouraged to discuss with you whenever he feels the "ghost in the room" so that you can become more aware of when your child (and maybe even you) are letting the past take center stage. Sometimes while it is obvious to others, for you and your children it might just happen almost seamlessly because the past is still so much of who all of you are.

- Try not to personalize a child's need to talk about the deceased parent. (You might suggest he remember that it has nothing to do with him, but everything to do with the difficulty of letting go.)

Most critical, it is important that there is an understanding established between you and your new partner that the lost parent cannot be banished but has a place in the present. Ideally, eventually, references to her can flow in and out with relative ease, becoming woven gently into the creation of new experiences. If you are at the beach with your children and your new love, it should be okay for your children to note, "Mom used to love the waves." And it would be great if your partner could say, "It must have been so much fun to enjoy them with her." Because chances are it was and children will appreciate the acknowledgement of a very important memory. This is something that both you and your new partner need to project together so that your children can see this new person is not a replacement. Nor is she closing any emotional doors.

But she is someone who can open many others.

Your children will only allow this gift to happen in their lives if they have *permission* to speak their minds.

Shrines and Altars

Dating a person who prominently displays highly charged memorabilia belonging to a deceased spouse can be extraordinarily difficult. Asking that a few things be "put away" can sound dangerously like "get past it already." However, it's important to make it clear that what is meant is "please give me some room to step in."

You have been dating Larry, who was widowed two years ago and has a seven-year-old daughter named Allison. Your relationship has been progressing into serious territory, but unfortunately, you feel as if you are sharing that territory with his deceased wife. There are pictures of her everywhere. Certainly you know that Allison cannot or should not be expected to simply put aside the past. Allison also

has possessions of her mother's that she occasionally leaves about the house—her comb, her shawl, and other personal items. But here too you realize these are concrete reminders and they are good for her.

However, in the master bedroom there is an eight-by-ten resting on the night table. You've been biding your time about when to tell him this is bothering you. You desperately haven't wanted to seem insensitive.

Now it is a Friday evening and you will be spending the weekend at Larry's while Allison is off at her grandparents. You arrive with a small bag and upon opening a drawer of his bureau you find his deceased wife's things still there. Her intimate things. In fact, you can still catch a scent . . . and you have had enough.

It's a funny thing about shrines. They can just happen. The surviving family members have consciously or unconsciously decided to keep the deceased person's belongings exactly as they were . . . as if to freeze time.

But freezing time is the last thing you want. Enjoying every moment of your new relationship is more to the point. Still you will have to face that Larry has elected to keep his deceased wife's things in place. You will need to understand what exactly this choice means for him, keeping in mind it was also his choice to build a relationship with you. When you speak with Larry it will be most important to understand the degree of ambivalence he must be experiencing, and to speak of your own.

Dating a widow or widower can give anyone pause if they feel as if they are drowning in memories and memorabilia. Bringing this experience to your lover's attention can actually serve to awaken him to the full present reality.

"Larry," you might begin. "I have to tell you I don't expect you to simply forget that you had a wife who you loved very much. But I am growing increasingly more uncomfortable with the multitude of pictures in the house and the many things of hers you still keep in the drawers. I feel as if I'm being haunted. Can you tell me what's going on for you?"

Hopefully a partner will be able to see what you are saying immediately but many will not. The same denial that has kept the deceased spouse's things sitting about the house could stand in the way of any easy self-insight.

"I'm just saving things for Allison. It's no big deal," Larry says.

This is a tough one. He's put it on Allison—the one person for whom pulling back on the pictures or material items would clearly be a difficult problem.

"But she cannot see the things in your bureau drawer," you say gently. You need to confront him to see if he is indeed available at all for a true relationship.

Larry looks at you for a long, quiet moment, and both of you know that the point has been made. "I'm sorry," he says sadly. "It's been so difficult." For the next half hour he proceeds to tell you how hard it's been to let someone new into his life, in a way that he has never spoken about it before. He ultimately agrees it's time to put away a few pictures and to pack up his wife's things.

You are thrilled, but the two of you know that it's not going to be simple because from Allison's perspective any removal of an item that reminds her of her mother could feel like an attack.

A child who hangs onto "things" is also trying to hold on to the love she has had for her mother. A change in decor or the possibility of loving someone else could feel as if it might threaten her ability to keep the past in the present. The two of you agree that Larry will talk to Allison alone. It has been clear to both of you that though Allison loved her mother she has also craved attention and companionship from you. She dearly wants another person to mother her here on earth. You've polished her nails, giggled and cuddled together and she is definitely attached. To involve yourself in the conversation could possibly feel as if you and her father have plotted together to remove memories of her mother.

One evening over a quiet dinner Larry said, "You know, Allison, I've been thinking. I love having Mom's things around, but sometimes I have the feeling that they keep me feeling sad. She wouldn't like that at all. I'm wondering if they aren't doing the same for you. Maybe we could put away just a few pictures, and some of Mom's stuff."

"I want them to stay where they are," Allison answered forcefully.

But Larry pressed on, insisting that he was quite sure her mother wouldn't mind. He walked around the house with Allison, pointing out just how many remembrances there were. Allison kept saying, "But I like that picture," at every turn. Then, just as Larry was about to give up Allison tearfully admitted she was afraid that if they removed *anything* her mother would think they didn't care anymore.

Larry, he tells you later, froze for a few minutes, for he too had these feelings. But as a result of this he was able to come up with a compromise.

"How about if we start slowly," he suggested. "And you can help make the choices of which picture we might put away, or which item we might pack up? We'll see how it feels, and if it's okay, maybe select a few other things. . . ." Allison jumped at this idea so quickly Larry got the feeling somehow she'd been wanting to do this as well.

When next you visited you wondered whether Allison would make the connection between you and the slightly altered decor, and in fact she did. Pointing to a picture on the side table that had been switched from her mother to her puppy, Allison said, "We decided to use some different pictures."

You nodded. "You have the cutest puppy, Allison," you reply. "I know Mom's picture used to sit here, but I can still see her in the picture over the piano." You do this purposefully. In order for Allison to begin to let go she has to know she can still do some hanging on and that the world around her still recognizes her love for the lost parent. In embracing Allison's memories yourself, she will be more inclined to move toward and not away from you.

As for the picture next to the bed, you noticed shortly after your first discussion that it disappeared. You decide not to mention it. Larry is an adult and he doesn't need your affirmation of his love for his deceased wife. He needs you to affirm life instead.

"My Kids Are My Date"

When a beloved spouse dies children can provide shelter. They share your pain and know what you miss. They can also be a lifeboat. But as with all lifeboats, while at first you are grateful to have them, at some point you're going to need to get off and get back to life.

After your wife died, you were at a low ebb. Fortunately you run your own business so your time was your own. Unfortunately you were treating your time as if it wasn't worth much. You prepared school lunches for your eight-year-old son and ten-year-old daughter, picked them up, hired someone to take them to their activities, and managed to squeeze some work in between. But mostly the three of you stuck together like traumatized army buddies. Gradually as the pain subsided you became a happier trio, bonding in ways you never had before. Now you shop and cook together, watch videos, garden; you are a tight domestic dream team.

Your children seem pleased to draw you right into their worlds, which is exactly what you need, a way out of your own mournful one. You cling to each other in a sort of cocoon. It feels good. Of course in the back of your mind, you have felt that maybe you were becoming too tight, too over-involved. But the volume on your concern is turned down low because you want to stay in this safe place. Maybe you fear they will vanish as your wife had vanished in the car accident. She drove away one day and never came back. You hold a quiet terror inside.

But now suddenly, an outside observer is telling you what you already knew. You've just attended your daughter's school conference during which time her teacher lets you know that Ellen was overly occupied with how you were doing. Her interest in close friends seemed to be dissipating, and did you know she was thinking of dropping out of after-school soccer?

You feel stunned . . . but more because you know the time has come to regroup the troubled troops, and you aren't at all sure you're ready.

Sitting there in front of the teacher you felt overwhelmed with guilt, suddenly hearing loud and clear what you had known: The family had gotten too insulated and enclosed and you had led the way. Clearly, your daughter has been following your lead. She sensed your fear and need and it amplified her own fear of losing the only parent she has. She had clearly decided to protect you, watch over you, and never let you out of her sight unless she had to. But now it is time to get your kids back into the swing of a healthy life. Matt has kept to his sports, you think to yourself with relief, but even he was not fighting for play dates. It was time for them to address their own needs. You would have to get to yourself later.

Your opportunity comes very soon. That evening an old friend of Ellen's called inviting her for a sleepover. You heard your daughter say she could come for a few hours but not sleep over and before you could stop her she hung up.

"It's okay," Ellen said, misunderstanding your concerned expression. "Don't worry, I'm not going to stay overnight there."

You know this is your chance to reverse the tide. You take a deep breath. "It's been a long time since you have just hung out with your friends. You always enjoyed them so much. You and Jessica were always together." You pause and offer up what you hope will be the magic key. "She was a girl that Mommy liked too."

"I think I should come home," Ellen says, clearly not buying it.

Matt, who you hadn't noticed was listening and suddenly you hear him pipe up, "I like it better when Ellen is home too."

You look from child to child sadly. "We've got to talk." You realize that you are ready for this conversation. Maybe you've been getting ready to retrieve some independence as well. You tell them what you think has been happening.

"We have all been so good at being supports for each other. I think the support should and needs to continue, there are other ways to do it than to always be together. It's time to create a new way of being a family, which includes spending some time away from each other and then coming together again to catch up." You almost add, "It's time to get back to normal" but of course there isn't any normal that is available now. Their mother has died and it would be foolish to speak as if any of you could return to a previous state. "Mommy's death shocked all of us and has made us cling to one another and I've really been the worst one about it. I think I've made you afraid that something else bad would happen."

"Sometimes I think that something could happen," Matt said.

You nod, relieved that Matt is letting it out. "Look, anything could happen but it isn't likely. We lived all these years being just fine and we have to live assuming the best, otherwise, we won't have any fun. We'd all hate that and Mom would *really* be angry at that! I want us all to get into our individual lives again. Sitting around and holding on to one another every chance we get won't keep all bad things away. It's not that we replace the old people but we can leave room to enjoy other people who are here now and available to love and be loved."

"But you'll be lonely," Ellen says.

You're not sure which one of you she is really talking about and so you take it from both perspectives.

"Sweetie, I'm a little lonely even when you guys are around. But I'll be happier if I know you're having a good time. And Ellen, if you allow yourself to really start enjoying your friends again, I think you'll feel happier too."

Both children are quiet and look a bit dubious. Something else is necessary. Suddenly it comes to you. "Let's talk about the ways we can stay close even if we aren't with each other."

"We could call each other on the phone!" Ellen suggests. "We could agree to have Saturday lunches together," Matt offers. "Neither of us have practice then." Then you offer you own suggestion and in a commanding way so that they know you are going to make sure the three of you stick together. "We all *must* have Sunday dinner together. Period!"

You can see the children relax right before your eyes.

Later that night you realize you've missed one piece to this new life plan. And that's you. You have to start stepping out as well. You have to make a new adult life. With trepidation, you accept the number of the sister of a woman who you work with and make plans to take her to lunch. The two of you fail to click but you try again with someone else. This time it's rather nice and one evening, you actually make sure that Ellen has a sleepover planned out of the house. She calls to say good night and you are in great spirits, reassuring her that she does not have to worry about you. If your kids experience you as being fine, they will worry about you less.

It is easy to fall into the safe routine of relying on the kids. Their fears and anxieties and sense of loss can dovetail so well with your own that it can seem like a perfect fit. Unfortunately if it goes on too long it becomes the perfect "pit." Their job is to move out in the world and be with peers, gain new skills, pursue interests, and find out who they are within (yes, that's part of it) and outside of this family. You have to get a life so that you can move on and they can see you do it.

The point here is each of you have boundaries that deserve protection. You want these boundaries to be strong enough so that the three of you can stay close, but not so fused or enmeshed that no one can separate from the other. Children, even grieving ones, grow healthfully when they can go out into the world knowing they have a secure, stable home to which they can return. This is true for younger children as well. It would be very detrimental to a seven-year-old's emotional growth to unconsciously fill her with trepidation each time she's tempted to go off with a friend. A simple "Great. You'll have such a good time" will help to keep her on track and strengthen her belief that she can be safe without you by her side. Grieving spouses will begin to move through their pain as they too allow themselves to go out, while knowing that the family unit is solidly in place. In other words each of you will do best if you can recognize that belonging to each other is something that will not dissipate as you go your separate ways. Quite to the contrary, letting each other have a good time only reinforces your devotion.

"We Want You to Be Happy"

Twenty-year-olds may look and sound almost like adults, but when it comes to you and your dating life the five-year-old who resides within may suddenly emerge. This is partly because of their life stage. Ready and not ready to leave home, twenty- to twenty-five-year-olds can present a very confusing picture: at once grasping for independence and your apron with equal passion.

Your husband died after a short illness when you were forty-eight years old. You had been married for twenty-two years. You were devastated. Your girls were twenty and eighteen. For about two years the three of you helped each other through, weeping, hugging, and laughing together, even long-distance as the two girls went off to college. Now it's almost two years after his death and at long last you're feeling the need to rebuild your emotional life. Your oldest, Jen, living at home after finishing college, sensed this first and started to encourage you to become more social. You knew you needed to but it had been so long since you first dated that you couldn't imagine doing anything about it. Besides the idea that your husband might be able to look down and see you "catting around" alternately seemed horrible and hysterical. In short, you didn't know whether to laugh or cry. But your determined daughter, Jen, now twenty-two, started to bring pamphlets home for you to look at: grief groups, parents without partners groups, continuing education classes, the works. After about one month of this constant bombardment you decided to join a widow/widower group. You had to laugh. The very first night out an attractive widower flirted with you. It felt pretty darn good. After a few meetings, he asked you out to see a show and you accepted.

You came home that evening and proudly told Patti, your youngest, who happened to be home from her senior year in college, of your conquest. She smiled softly and said, "Congrats, Mom." You could tell she meant it though there was some sadness there. Jen walked in shortly thereafter from yet another apartment-hunting mission and you announced your news.

It was as if you'd told her the laundry was done. Her affect was as flat as a pancake. "That's great," she intoned.

Most young adults between the ages of eighteen and twenty-five carry with them the vestiges of neediness and dependence they had when they were younger. They have more mature imaginations. They can conceive of the notion that Mom shouldn't be living her life alone forever but when you say, "Hey, what about me," and, "Isn't this my time?" they don't really get it. This is a confusing life-stage time for young adults and a newly dating parent is bound to add to their fears and anxieties about "what's next."

You had thought Jen would be the most excited by your news. She is the one who'd waged a campaign for you to get out there and find love. Yet you also knew upon hearing of your exploits her response was not sincere and that her expression revealed some deep concern.

You asked her what was wrong. "Honey, I thought this is what you wanted me to do. I thought we both kind of agreed it was time for me to get out there. Why do you look so . . . well . . . annoyed?"

"Don't make a big thing, Mom, I was just in a bad mood; there's nothing more to it, really," Jen answers.

You have a funny feeling there might be something competitive going on here. You know Jen has been struggling to find her feet as an independent person, and here you are taking strides to be just that. Was it possible she could really only stand one of you in that position right now?

You didn't speak of it again to Jen, though you did say a few words to Patti, who, while looking a bit uncomfortable, still appeared genuinely pleased for you. You also made a point of asking Jen about how she was liking her new job (she wasn't) and how the apartment hunt was going (it wasn't). You began to get the feeling she was having trouble leaving home.

A few weeks later, you invited Jerry over to the house while Jen was supposed to be out with some friends for the evening. She got in while you and Jerry were having some ice cream so you asked her if she'd like to join you. Suddenly Jerry slipped his arm around your waist. You winced. Jen agreed politely to ice cream, her eyes glued to his hand. The minute she sat down at the table it started: "Remember when Dad always sat in this chair? Remember, Mom, the old maroon chair pad that he had forever?" You acknowledged it weakly to dissuade her from going on but she was on a roll. She turned to Jerry. "Dad liked to fish, Dad liked to refinish furniture . . . do you like any of that stuff?"

You were dumbfounded. You'd heard of this kind of thing happening with younger kids, but from the mouth of a twenty-two-year-old? Had you been totally off base about her wanting to be independent? Was her behavior a delayed reaction to the finality of her father's death?

The likelihood is "yes" to both.

Your eldest daughter actually isn't quite ready to move on, even though intellectually she knows this is how things have to be. The new man in her mom's life is signaling the absolute truth that her dad is gone. Her enthusiasm for you to date had been genuine as she knew staying vibrant and finding love was your best option for happiness. But what she had known (knows) in her head doesn't quite match what is in her heart. All of this is complicated by her life stage. This is a time for her to be working toward leaving the nest and finding her own way. But not only must she do this while you are seemingly leaving the nest too, but you're doing it first! Fortunately, Jerry was patient with the constant references to your deceased husband. You also worked hard to help Jen understand you were still her mother, and a person to fall back on while she struggled to find the right job and a nice apartment. You made sure to be available for advice and would also occasionally talk about Jerry in a way that let her know her father was still on your mind. At one point Jen asked, "Do you let Jerry touch you?" You hesitated. Certainly you did but somehow a yes or no did not seem like an adequate answer—or actually not the one for which Jen was really asking. "Jerry and I like each other a lot and sometimes we are very close, but you know I'll never forget how it was with Dad." Patti, you noticed, seems more relaxed and thoughtful now.

"Jerry and I went to a concert at the town hall last night. It was a concert Dad would have liked," you say softly while you're sitting in the living room with Jen. What was played? Jen wanted to know. And so you told her and each of you mused how much her father and your husband had enjoyed Mozart. "I missed Dad listening to the music," you added. Jen nodded solemnly . . . and then she did what people in confused and ambivalent states will do. She said, "Oh, well, I hope Jerry liked it also?"

You were thrilled. Apparently Jen had gotten something from you she still needed to know even at age twenty-two. You still love her father, you still think of her father, and you still miss him, just as she does. Gradually after this conversation, Jen's references to her father in front of Jerry began to lessen. Once when Jerry was coming to dinner and she suggested making what you both knew was her father's favorite meal, you looked at her cross-eyed. Jen was actually able to laugh. Occasionally you mention her father, saying something like, "Jerry is great, but I have to say it does feel odd dating someone other than your dad!"

Jen always has a melancholy look on her face when you say something like this but you sense the moment is good for her. It's a chance for her to allow herself to feel sad and know that she is not alone with those feelings.

"Matchmaker, Matchmaker, Don't Make Me a Match"

Some children, anxious to end your apparent loneliness (and their sense of responsibility for it) may decide it's time to take matters into their own hands. Unfortunately they may tend to view anyone who is available as dating material. It matters little who he is . . . but rather that he's alone. It's touching that your child may want to look out for you—and it's important to be appreciative—but it's equally important to say, "This is part of my life I can handle on my own" (even if you don't believe it!).

After your husband died, you had to go back out to work. Jack had left you in reasonable financial shape but you were only forty, and the money wasn't going to last forever. You took a sales job at a gift shop and it was okay. Your twelve-year-old daughter, however, seemed to blossom with the new responsibilities your working life imposed upon her. It was quite impressive. She had been accustomed to you being there when she got home from school, but she turned into a latchkey kid with nary a complaint. You were very proud of how she took on the new responsibilities and did them well. Sometimes she even got dinner ready all by herself, which was something you had never asked her to do. You of course urged your daughter to go out as much as possible and after a while she did and you were pleased to see her enjoy her friends . . . though you were beginning to feel almost jealous. It was a coupled world out there and you were always feeling out of place when you joined old friends. You made the mistake of telling this to Cathy.

You didn't realize you'd just hired Cathy for a new job.

About a week after your admission, Cathy told you that she had a surprise planned and that you should look nice on Friday when you got home from work. You thought maybe you'd end up going to the diner instead of eating in.

You arrived home to find Cathy, her friend Amy, and Amy's father all waiting to have dinner with you. Amy's dad was divorced and the girls had lured him over to cheer you up. He was a good sport. Secretly, the girls had hoped the two of you would fall in love and they could be sisters for real. "I knew this would make you happy, Mom," Cathy said, heaping a big pile of spaghetti onto your plate. You smiled, not wanting to hurt her feelings. Mr. Malone was pleasant enough, a nice, lonely single man. But he wasn't for you. After the shock wore off, you managed to get through the evening with an embarrassed, frozen smile.

If this event hadn't been such an eye-opener to the fact that your fatigue, depression, and grieving had resulted in you abdicating all grown-up responsibilities so that your twelve-year-old felt the need to take on the role of social director, housekeeper, and mother, you would have found it funny.

It was time, you knew, to get out of bed literally and figuratively and take care of not only your daughter's life, but your own. It was time to be the adult.

As you closed the door at the evening's end, Cathy said, "He's cool, Mom, isn't he? Do you like him? I think he liked you."

"Cathy, this was the sweetest thing that you could have done, a real act of love. But you know you didn't have to do this. I feel like you've been doing too much."

Cathy shrugged, "It's okay, Mom." You noticed she didn't argue.

"It's not okay, I am the mother and it's been hard since Daddy died to want to do anything; I think it scared you to see me so low all the time."

"I guess, yeah, I guess." Cathy looked down.

"I'm sorry, I'm going to try to change. I am the mother here though I must say you have done a wonderful job of trying to be a matchmaker." You pause. "But I think I need to start doing that for me. Finding my own dates is my job." You stroke her cheek. "You want me to pick out your boyfriends?"

"Yuck!!" Cathy answered without skipping a beat. You both looked at each other and started laughing hysterically.

After the "matchmaker" dinner, you forced yourself to get some help with a counselor. You needed support to get back up. It was not your child's role to keep you vertical. You hadn't grieved your husband, and you had gotten stuck in sadness and self-pity. You still feel it and want to take to your bed sometimes but you don't get as stuck for as long. Cathy sees you being less sad and this frees her up to get back into her kid life. As for Martin, you didn't become a couple but rather, warm acquaintances. You did, however, have a coffee with a guy from work. It's a start. A new start.

EVERYONE grieves in different ways and over differing amounts of time. There is no right or wrong moment to begin dating again . . . as long as you do indeed finally do so. Your child may not be operating on your schedule. If he isn't ready for you to date then at least for a while do so out of view—recognizing that you cannot hide a growing relationship for long. Your child will simply have to cope and likely, as a consequence, begin to embrace life in a more fuller way himself.

As for all those pictures and other memorabilia, it might be a nice idea, as you begin to put a few things away, to frame photographs of you and your children either alone or with a new special person. Place them one by one around the house as well, but try to remember to choose places where perhaps a ceramic bowl had previously sat and not a picture of the deceased. This new life is not a replacement. It's the future.

8

Mature Dating: Aren't You a Little . . . Old?

JUST when you thought life would be smooth sailing, it isn't. The children are finally out on their own. Whatever shape their lives have taken, you have done your part to get them to a place where they can meet their own needs and take care of themselves. You may be recently divorced. You may be divorced for many years or widowed and desirous of a companion. No matter where you are however, you believe you are free of the watchful eyes of your children. They live on their own and you live on your own. What difference could your dating or sex life make to them now?

A parent's dating, coupling, and remarrying will have an effect on their children no matter how old they are or what they are doing in their own lives. For children, any time their parent bonds with someone other than the original parent they are going to have feelings and reactions. It's a fact that once you have children, there are no longer clean breakups, endings, or beginnings.

You may have many anxieties and concerns as well. Can you successfully date again? How will a new life combine or blend with the old one? Will everyone get along? You understand your needs but you may suspect your children will find it . . . bizarre. You may sense with vague or acute awareness that your children are watching you. As a single man or woman, you may deeply want companionship but it can be threatening when it comes at the expense of alienating your children or feeling alienated yourself.

Kids, We're Getting a Divorce

You call your children and tell them you and their dad are getting a divorce. The truth is you've both been wanting to do this for a long time and you were quite sure it would come as no surprise to your kids. But you're met with a stony silence. An hour later there's a tearful young adult standing on your doorstep. "How . . . how could you?" she is sputtering.

Your first reaction may be incredulousness. For goodness sake, this daughter has been out of the house for a few years. She has her own life. A live-in boyfriend. A budding career.

But the truth is in some ways we all take our homes with us—for better or for worse. Yes, it may have been a source of problems but hopefully it was also a source of love and support. Adult children often want to call upon their childhood homes for strength—the security, the love, the predictability will comfort them as they move through their lives whether or not they are actually physically there. They carry their homes in their hearts, and if the home breaks up they can feel as if their touchstone is vanishing.

They will need time to process that the shape of this "rock" in their lives is changing. Let your children cry, be angry or sullen. Adult children will often return to childhood patterns. Or if they don't they may still need, in some more mature form, evidence of a deep caring and abiding love from their parents. Adult children, in short, still need anchors.

The best and only thing you can do is communicate that the "hearth" they counted on, you and your husband, is inside them.

It may no longer exist as the entity they knew but the essence remains.

Of course if one parent suddenly ups and leaves the other parent, *huge* conflicts in loyalties can surface. Children are old enough to understand how hard it might be for one or both of you to find other mates. They may feel that the parent leaving is being wildly selfish yet feel great love for him or her.

Although the children are grown, it's best to treat this the same way you would have had they been younger.

Taking sides does nothing but tear families apart. Heart-to-hearts with your children as to why all of this is taking place might be appropriate but you don't want to overload them with the intimacies of your marriage.

If there is another relationship afoot, immediately bringing her into the picture won't easily fly. Even grown-up kids might see her as an interloper and her presence may stir up profound feelings of loss and in some circumstances great protectiveness for one parent or another. In other words, the family balance will be akimbo for quite some time. It would be unreasonable to expect otherwise and so your grown-up children should be allowed the time to work through their own feelings . . . even though you may be tempted to snap, "Grow up!"

Feeling Self-Conscious in Front of the Kids

When your marriage of over twenty years broke up, it was the start of the holiday season. You began spending some time with a woman from work. Both of you were being careful not to jump into a rebound relationship, so you developed a friendship, allowing the obvious chemistry and sexual tension to flicker in the background. You were thinking you might bring her over to your daughter and son-in-law's house for Christmas day, but as the holidays grew ever nearer you began feeling uneasy. You could all too easily imagine your children scrutinizing this woman, comparing her to their mother—a veritable tribe of detectives trying to discern your girlfriend's failings.

If you are on your own and dating, you need only concern yourself with your own feelings toward this new person. But as soon as you imagine your children in the same room this will change, even if your children do or say nothing! You may feel oddly distant from the new life you are trying to build. Seeing your children, and perhaps their mother, will bring visions of past occasions that can seem to leave no room for a new person and your feelings for her. After all, there are no memories between you, your children, and this new person. There is no common ground or shared history to rely upon.

Hopefully, reality will set in. You got divorced in order to move forward. The past will always be there as rich as before. It needn't interfere with your ability to enjoy the present and look forward to a new life and new memories.

You may notice a turned-up nose on one of your children or a quick shake of the head by another. Or you might see one child pouring on the attention and wondering if it's for real. That's all right. Unlike with younger children, you don't have to worry about the relationship they will build with this person. A level of cordiality is adequate and if more blossoms that would be wonderful.

Self-consciousness in front of your children means you are in many ways looking for approval that you don't need. Certainly they love you but they will form opinions based on protectiveness, their own ability to accept you as a sexual being, and also, still, loyalty to the other parent. Try and let them grapple with these issues without letting it worry you.

What the Children See and What the Children Miss

Older children may experience your dating as a betrayal and an act of disloyalty to the family . . . or to be more exact, the family history. Whenever you show up with your date or partner, they may not only get a visceral hit of the sadness and loss, but they may experience this new person's presence as an intrusion on their life story.

Unfortunately, older children have less opportunity to witness the affection, intimacy, and dynamics between you and a significant other once they are out of the house. They also have less of an opportunity to look beyond their own needs and recognize how importantly yours are being filled. They may see you together mostly in social settings so they are not experiencing the degree to which this "other" relationship is enriching your life. They can only see it's changing the canvas of their life story in a way that doesn't feel right.

If the parents are divorced and a new relationship is serious, the protocol for holidays and important events becomes an issue. One dad was asked by his adult children not to come to Thanksgiving with a woman he had been dating for over a year because it would be "too upsetting for his ex-wife." The parents had been divorced for several years but it still felt too awkward and upsetting to have everyone together—although it was unclear who was more uncomfortable, the children or the ex-wife. This barrier in families with adult children is common. Married children of divorce almost never see both parents together on a holiday. For most people, mixing the new with the old is too charged. This means that children of divorce are forever having to negotiate around which parent can come to what and where they can sit and which holiday it's best to leave town altogether in order to avoid the whole mess.

That Thanksgiving the dad resolved to see his adult children with his girlfriend the day after the holiday. It seemed like the best solution but the dad felt deprived of being with his children, his girlfriend was hurt, his ex-wife felt guilty but relieved, and the children later reported it was a thrill not to have to figure out which ones of their children would be "sick" so that they would have to leave early.

One dad who was remarrying said to his twenty-seven-year-old daughter, with disbelief, "You should be happy for me." All she could think about was that her mother was going into her golden years alone. It wasn't until her mother remarried a few years later that the daughter could feel relieved and happy for both of her parents.

What About Us?

Sometimes parents decide it's time to make a big geographical change with their new companion.

"I was very excited when my sixty-four-year-old mother met and fell in love with Fred. He was a lovely man, educated and interesting and loved to travel. She lost my dad when he was sixty and had been alone ever since. I was thirty-nine, married, and had two kids. They were very nice together and it felt right . . . that is until they announced that they were buying a home two thousand miles away."

Many adult children of dating parents find that they can accept the new life that their parent chooses. However, when the change significantly alters the life they have become accustomed to (Mom lives a half hour away), it can be a jolt. The old visceral "I want my Mommy" pulls on everyone's heart strings. When you love someone very much, any major separation or any significant change will call into question how the distance will alter your relationship. If a parent moves far away, the adult child who has always felt a strong attachment to him or her might actually feel frightened or abandoned. This is an opportunity for the adult child to examine those ties and to perhaps loosen them a bit to promote his or her own sense of competence.

A parent experiencing their adult child's insecurity may be tempted to stay put—to not "abandon" a loved one. But it is important to keep in mind that one of the greatest things any parent can give a child is faith in himself and his own abilities. If it didn't completely happen as this adult child grew up, now's your chance.

Reworking Expectations

No matter how many times we hear about the divorce rate, the number of stepfamilies, and the complexities of families in general, children and adults hope for simple happy endings.

Getting real about expectations is the healthiest approach to new relationships—yours and others. Looking at what is possible is more helpful than pushing for what you want when the people involved are not necessarily going to be capable of jumping through the hoop. Look at it from your child's perspective. Your dad wants you to feel close to his new partner. You're an adult now and have a whole reservoir of communication skills and perspectives that a young child in a divorced home has not yet developed. You have a greater capacity to be social, conciliatory, and the maturity to delay your needs and sort them out in relation to others. It should be easier for everyone to know and like each other. Sometimes it's not. Maybe you can allow yourself to see who this new person is, and find places where you can share feelings and thoughts and enjoy genuine compatibility. On the other hand, maybe you just don't like him, or you feel too much loyalty to your other parent to even give it much of a try. Sure, you're old enough to act polite and dutiful but that's not the same as being truly open to a new person even if your parent wants you to be.

When partnering anew after your children are adults, everyone's different needs will spring to the surface. When children are little and more dependent, they need to have adults nurture them and work to create a dynamic in the home that is warm and comfortable. This is not only a loving goal, but a practical one. Children and adults do need to find a way to live together peacefully. However, as an adult, you have a separate life, where you can feel free to meet your own emotional needs in any way you wish. Your hopes can extend to wanting your loved ones to like your new mate. But to place your expectations there might be a problem.

One aspiring actress said, "I resisted my stepmother for a few years. She was a pleasant enough person but I felt guilty about my mother so I kept the relationship cool. Then I realized that I respected her a great deal. She was a set designer and offered to help me make some connections for my acting career. I accepted her help and got to know who she was as a person aside from all the family entanglements and I discovered I liked her as a friend."

These two people came together because they found their own way.

"I turned forty-two this year and my mother remarried nine years ago. I still refer to my stepfather as the other man. We've always been distant; we're different kinds of people. She always hoped we'd have some male bonding but it will never happen."

Accepting the lack of connection is the easiest road to not quite tension-free but acceptable get-togethers.

Dating in Tandem

Some adult children of divorced and widowed parents find themselves on the quest to find a mate at the same time as their mother or father.

One mother and daughter found themselves at the same event in their small community. "It was so weird—this guy who was standing with my mother and much closer to her age than mine started to flirt with me," a thirty-two-year-old said. "Fortunately we laughed about it and could commiserate on how difficult it can be to find the right match. He wasn't right for either of us." Other times when this mother and daughter were at the same event, they had to encourage one another to move around the room and mingle. "Listen," her mother would say, "Don't follow me around, go and do what you came to do, meet new people." Another time her mother offered, "I don't see anyone for me but there are two interesting guys for you."

This tandem dating situation can also inspire unexpected feelings. Jealousy is one.

A forty-year-old wondered how she would feel if her widowed dad found a partner before she did. She figured she'd be happy for him while at the same time feel competitive: "No fair, he already had a full marriage, I haven't even been able to find one yet."

An adult child might also feel as though she is losing a shoulder to cry on. If she can't find a date and neither can Mom, it's harder for her to commiserate. If a son has a broken heart and his mother has also been recently ditched, he may not feel good about unloading himself to her.

In most circumstances children hope and expect their parents will be one step ahead of the game. They will want their parents to be wise. They will hope you are a rock. If an adult child has dug a hole for himself he will want to know that, if he needs to, he can draw on a parent's strength. If you're both dating together he's more likely to feel it's a case of the blind leading the blind . . . which at the very least can feel disconcerting.

As the parent, it might be wise, as much as possible, to highlight the differences in your situations so that if your child brings a problem to you he won't feel as if he's rubbing salt into a wound. "I'm just looking for someone to have fun with. You want a person who can be the one," you might say. "Sure, I feel dumped, but I've been around a long time. So many things have happened to me in the past that I can draw on to keep it in perspective. So let's talk."

There is an upside to tandem dating. Some parents who find themselves out in the dating world begin to empathize with their children's search. "It used to be that I nagged my daughter to get married and have children, but once I started dating after my twenty-year marriage ended and realized how tough it can be, I backed off. I finally understood what she had been telling me about how hard it is to meet someone." It is often startling to have to face a long struggle to find the love that you want. Unless one has this trying experience, it is often easy to dismiss the struggles of single people and insist the quest can't be *that* difficult.

Love Consultants, Ltd.

One mother who had not ventured into the dating world for some twenty-nine years was unseasoned and unskilled in reading particular cues from men. When her mother would describe a flirtatious interaction, her daughter was surprised and concerned about her mom's naivete. "Some of these men found my mom attractive but really were only interested in flings, and my mother didn't realize it until I clued her in. She was completely out of practice and I had to decode signals for her that I had been dealing with for years."

Some support, love, and understanding is wonderful if a child can be available. However, if a child becomes the major confidant for a parent it can feel "too close for comfort." It is necessary to keep good boundaries about what one can and can't ask for and expect between parents and children. Keeping a neutral perspective can be hard to do with anyone you care for so deeply. Parents can get caught up "just wanting my daughter to be happy." Children can find themselves wishing "my mom could find someone to take care of her." Advice can quickly lose its objectivity. Each family has their own comfort zone around intimacy, but the parental relationship is not the same as a relationship with a friend. There can be too much talking in detail, too much worrying about the outcome of each pursuit because parents and children have a major stake and are greatly affected and influenced by each other's choices and happiness.

What Are You Going to Do with Mother's Things?

Your children will hopefully make peace with a divorce or death. Coping with the loss of hearth and home is also doable . . . but it may not include everything in it. These tangibles that represent "home" are very precious and can appear to be at risk of disappearing if a widowed parent marries and puts a new person in the childhood home. Your children may not be able to help "asking," "Is this woman using my mother's set of dishes, lounging in her favorite chair, wearing jewels that she collected in her lifetime? Don't I have the right to possess these heirlooms left by my mother? Why does some stranger suddenly have more rights than flesh-and-blood children?"

Legally, your children have a reason to worry. It's awkward, because if the deceased parent does not specify possessions going to the children, they automatically go to the living spouse. If the living spouse does not share the values and views of his adult children, it can cause painful feelings and confrontations.

"My mother died before my father, and he remarried within six months. This called into question matters of the inheritance. My mother had always intended to make a separate will for the two of us, my brother and myself, but she was afraid of hurting my dad and so when she passed away, everything of hers came under his jurisdiction. If he didn't specify particular valuables going to us, his new wife would basically have possession of my mother's and for that matter my father's entire heritage."

This family was under huge tension around this issue. The dad couldn't deal with his own mortality and so kept avoiding facing the task of making a will, which created huge problems between the new wife and the adult children. There was hurt and anger from the adult children toward their father for his failing to preserve what they deemed to be their right, at least to their mother's things. The adult children felt shut out and though they did not need financial assistance, they did need some material connection to their history.

In another family with a similar concern about a mother's legacy, a roundtable discussion took place. The adult children, the father, and the stepmother were able to air their feelings and wishes. Items that were sentimental and of great importance to a particular person were given to them. The father made provisions for his children and for his wife. The negotiations did not always run smoothly but the overall attitude of care and inclusion went a long way toward opening communication. By addressing the feelings and practical matters directly, the potential buildup of hurt, anger, resentment, fear, and worries was nipped in the bud.

The Will

Throughout our lives, children (and this includes adult children) look to their parents for protection. If you lose a job, become ill, or want to have a sense of being provided for, the family of origin is often the most common place for a child to turn, psychologically and practically. This is true even in families that have been emotionally disappointing. The last rung of the parental protection ladder is the inheritance. The adult asks, what provisions are made for me? And perhaps more deeply, how did my mother and father really feel about me? One mother who had had a very turbulent relationship with her children in the last five years of her life decided to leave everything to her second husband who nursed her through her final days. This was a painful legacy for her children, who felt traumatized by her anger at them and completely shut out because of the stepparent.

There are times when a parent involved in a long-term relationship that does not involve marriage passes on and makes no provisions for the partner with whom he shares a home. The children are left to consider their own inheritance in relation to this person. Because there is no legally binding agreement left by a deceased parent, the responsibility is left on the adult child's doorstep. Some adult children experience this as a coup while others are thrown into serious conflicts about what they want for themselves, what their parent might have wanted, and what they themselves think is fair to this other person.

Sad as it feels to focus on material items and cash at the end of a parent's life, such things become a lightening rod for discord when there is a remarriage or new significant other. Some adult children are quite focused on the possibility of being shut out or diminished considerably by a stepparent. Keep in mind that the desire for a part of a parent's estate is not only about cash but about what material items a child can connect to a parent for the rest of their journey through life. Sometimes one tattered book or a favorite watch that belonged to a mother or father will do. Respecting the emotional symbolism of possessions needs to be attended to by the parent left in charge.

The Relief of a Lucky Break

Many adult children feel relieved when their aging parent finds a partner. They report worrying about their parent being alone without companionship and though a new person does alter the home front and require some adjustments, it can feel better to know that a parent is enjoying life and being watched out for by someone other than oneself or other adult siblings. A companion for a parent sometimes makes the relationship with the parent emotionally safer. Mom or Dad are less needy now because their needs are being met elsewhere and they are not lonely anymore.

Other adult children who have an emotionally difficult relationship with a parent have found that a new amicable person can pave the way for a better experience. "My father is so hard to deal with and always was even when he and my mother were married, maybe especially when they were married. I find that my stepmother helps soften his rough edges and it's great. It makes seeing my dad easier. She's kind of fun sometimes."

One young woman whose mother passed away before she married was very lonely for a doting adult female. When her father remarried, she grew to enjoy her stepmother. The fact that her baby daughter had an active grandmother was truly helpful in filling her longings for her own mother. The warmth and affection of her stepmother completed and satisfied her need to have someone who was intimately interested in the details of her emotional life. It was a lucky break to find the closeness in the woman her father selected to be his partner.

9

Dating . . . with Children

MAKING new partners and children fit and function together is a complex and anxiety-provoking endeavor. Children question whether there will be more or less for them. Parents question how they can find love with a new adult while not forsaking their own children. As time passes divorced families will find their own way to preserve their ties and widows and widowers will find the room to let someone new into their lives.

The minute you became a parent you entered into a delicate negotiation between your needs and the needs of your child. When you left the child with a caretaker for a minute, an hour, a day, or a week in order to pursue the demands and desires of your individual self, somewhere inside you you were weighing the wisdom of that choice. How could you balance your desire to work out in the world, for instance, with your desire to parent and your child's need of you.

In many ways this dilemma faces you now . . . with the added burden of vigilant attention to your children's sense of loss and subsequent increased dependence upon you.

In your heart you know you cannot sacrifice your need for love. Nor would it be healthy to completely give yourself over to your children. It is extremely beneficial for them to see positive, loving behavior between a couple. It is an advantage for them to see conflicts resolved with love, care, and dignity. Observing adults who can express authentic feelings and use important personal social tools such as listening, understanding, empathizing, and honoring other individuals will bring immeasurable positive results to the family. This doesn't mean that everything works out to be near perfect all the time (when does it ever?), but what is lasting for children and for partners is the experience of genuine goodwill and love. Mending heartbroken spirits after a divorce or loss of a spouse through a death and offering your children the experience of finding and connecting to love again is one of the greatest gifts a parent can offer their children.

Building an emotional life with your children after divorce or death is a process. As you make this journey you will hit some bumps on the road but keep in mind the following:

- You can never push the timing of anyone's adjustment to new people. Each person has their own process, pacing, and ability to connect. Rhythms, temperaments, and skills are operating at similar and dissimilar levels and cannot be forced to move in a parallel way. *This is why it's important to introduce your dating life into the family slowly and carefully.*

- Everyone needs to feel that they have permission to experience whatever they are feeling without the fear of loss of love. Dismissing or diminishing anyone's thoughts and pains will not only stunt their ability to work them through and thus move past them, but it will also create an atmosphere of distrust. We all feel the safest with those who we trust will try to understand. *If your children are having trouble with your date, or the way in which the two of your show each other affection, encourage them to speak up. It's the easiest way to straighten out misunderstandings and clear the way for good feel-*

ings. Dating is a big deal. Expecting your children to easily go with the flow is unrealistic and asking them to sit on their resentful, fearful, or confused feelings is a sure road to difficult if not dangerous acting out.

- Children need to feel that the adults in their lives are available. They are in formative stages and phases and can't grow well without a hand. An adult's needs are critical but must always be balanced with those of your children if you have any hope of creating a new family life that abounds with a sense of security and love. *While you may at times be overwhelmed with a need to spend some passionate hours with a lover, it's important to stop and consider what your children might be going through. This is not to say you have to deny yourself pleasure . . . but rather that you have to time it in such a way that no one is paying a price because of it.*

- Demonstrate respect for everyone's personal boundaries. Guilt over a divorce or the pain your children experiences over a death can bring people together . . . sometimes too close. At first very close ties are natural. You are hanging on for comfort and to get your bearings. But then it will be time to loosen up. You can't depend on your children. *You need your own life and your children need to go back to theirs knowing you will all be okay. You need to keep those boundaries in place when it comes to your personal life. Children don't need to know about your sex life or the ins and outs of every relationship you try on for size. They won't like it or understand it, and as teenagers, may even be disgusted by it! You're a sexual human being. Good for you! But keep it between you, your lover, and trusted friends.*

The Last Note

Finding love again and making it work for your children is indeed a complex proposition. It is a journey that can be rewarding, enriching and quite beautiful. Try to allow this journey to happen organically. There is no one way either you or your children can or should react to the situations that lie ahead. The more detailed the expectations or picture you have in your head, the more disappointed you are bound to be. This won't be so because nothing is as good as you might like, but rather you will fail to notice the glorious connections and moments you never thought to imagine.

Try to be open. Enjoy sex and dating as a single parent, and let the feelings fall where they may. Respect, kindness, understanding, and patience will almost always win out.

Common Questions and Answers

> I had thought my eight-year-old son was fast asleep when my boyfriend and I slipped into bed to enjoy some lovemaking. We were quiet about it, as of course I was mindful that we were not alone in the apartment. All of a sudden, just as we were in the heat of things, Danny opened the bedroom door of our semi-darkened room and said, "Oh . . . I couldn't sleep." He looked as stunned as I felt. What should I have done, or do in the future?

Ask your child to return to his room and assure him that you will follow him in a moment. Then slip on a bathrobe or modest nightgown and quickly go to speak with him.

The first thing you will be wondering is, what did he see and what did it mean to him? Eight-year-olds vary in their knowledge of or interest in issues of sexuality. Some children will not have focused at all on the fact that you might have been having sex, but simply been surprised and confused to see your boyfriend with you in *your* room. Other children will know exactly what was going on and feel very embarrassed and confused by what they just saw. "My mom was doing it with Peter," he might think. "Yuck, and I saw it. I wish it would all just go away!"

Because you may not know for sure where your son rests in this spectrum it's a good idea not to immediately launch into a speech about what a man and woman do when they really like each other. And that's it's private. And that you thought he was asleep.

It will suffice to say, "I guess it surprised you to see Peter with me, huh?" Your child will likely nod.

"Well, we were just having some private time and I hope you weren't too surprised." To ask him if he was frightened or embarrassed might convey the idea that someone was doing something wrong and/or scary.

If your son nods and says something like, "Yeah. What is he still doing here?" and you are pretty sure he had at least seen you wrapped around each other, you might reply with honesty, "We were hugging and kissing. That's what we sometimes do but we didn't think you'd see us! It's a private thing and we probably shouldn't have been doing that while you were around. We should have been more careful!"

Here you're taking away any feeling that Peter might have done something wrong. You are also reassuring him that what he saw was lovely. (Sometimes a young person walking in on two adults making love can think someone is getting hurt.)

Then smile and assure him that the night will get back to normal. "Okay, look, let's get you tucked in. Peter is leaving in a few minutes anyway, and I'm going back to my room for a good night's sleep." Then kiss him good night, stay for a few minutes to see if he needs you, and then leave his room to bid your lover a fond adieu.

If the morning brings more questions, just say, "You know what? Peter and I were just having some affectionate private time. That's all."

Then quickly scramble the eggs.

My teenage daughter wanders in and sees me and my boyfriend, arms draped around each other, near midnight. She smiles and

says, "It's okay. You guys can sleep together here. I'm not going to mind." Should we?

The temptation will likely be to take your daughter at her word. After all, you two want to spend the night together. But remember you are dealing with a teen whose own hormones are raging, and who is going through the stage in which he or she is trying to create firm boundaries that you can't cross. Her words are surely a reflection of far more than her seeming desire to help you enjoy a healthy sex life—in fact, the thought of it, once she goes in her room and closes the door, might feel a lot more difficult than it did when she blithely gave you her permission.

Also, do you really want to conduct your sex life with a "papal dispensation" from your teenager? Do you want to give her that kind of power? Does she really want it? Is it good for any of you?

Your daughter should in no way feel that she can call the shots on this intimate part of your life. It's too much of an inappropriate responsibility. Deep down inside it's going to make her feel very uncomfortable because the sex life of any parent, to a teenager, is usually quite unfathomable. You will not want to give the impression that you need her "go-ahead" to be intimate. It's none of her business when you are or aren't. She should know that. She'll probably be relieved.

In a situation like this you will want to use a little humor and thank your daughter for "her permission" but explain you'll be parting this evening. You might add perhaps another time he'll stay over but say it in a way that reflects it's entirely your judgment call. "Thanks, honey, for giving us the go-ahead! But you know, we're not going to do that tonight. Perhaps another time though." Then smile and say, "Get a good night's sleep." Conversation over. Your teen may walk away with a cool shrug muttering something like, "Well it really wouldn't matter to me," in an effort to sound cool and grown-up. At this point you might sweetly call out, "This isn't about you!"

Weeks later when your boyfriend does sleep over, mention it to your teen and then keep moving. "Listen, Bob and I are going to be coming home later from a party so I think he'll be staying over. I didn't want you to be surprised in the morning."

This shows consideration for her feelings, respect for her rights in her own home, and your utter conviction that this decision is yours and yours alone to make.

> **My twelve-year-old son has taken a real liking to Charles, a guy I've been dating who lives nearby. The relationship is only two months old, but the other day my son knocked on his door to hand him an ad for a new car because they'd had a brief conversation about it when Charles had come to pick me up. Charles later commented to me he was a little uncomfortable being on those terms with my son so soon, and I didn't blame him. I also don't want him to feel pressured.**

It's difficult for kids to know their boundaries when it comes to you and your dates. This is especially true if it's a child who has need of the kind of companionship he "imagines" your date would be able to provide. A child might also insert himself into your relationship in this way because he's afraid of being "left out" or "forgotten." Whatever his reasons, the last thing you will want to do is embarrass or hurt him so you will need to tread carefully as you speak to him, making it clear he's done nothing wrong. It would also be wise to concentrate on how *you* feel about the incident rather than your date's impressions because to do otherwise might embarrass your child terribly.

At a nice, calm moment, you might say, "I heard you dropped off an interesting ad for Charles to see the other day." Your son may nod, perfectly relaxed. It was, he thinks, a fun thing to do. It felt good. He and Charles shared something.

"You know, I think it's great that you like Charles, honey," you might say, "and I think he found the ad very informative. But do you think you could hold off from visiting him again? It's not about Charles. It's about me. I'm not sure if we're going to continue dating, although we might, and I wouldn't want you to feel attached to him and then have to give that up. It's one thing to chat with him when he comes here to pick me up, it's another to visit him at his house. . . ."

"It was just an ad," your son says a bit defensively, completely oblivious to some of the complex and unconscious reasons he might have stopped by to see Charles.

"Yes, I know, but it's not the ad, honey," you might say. "It's you seeing Charles on your own that I'm worried about. I'm sure he enjoyed what you gave him, but I would prefer that you keep what happens between you to our house, or when I am with the two of you. If that changes I'll let you know."

My wife had been sick for many years and died. For the last year or so she'd been completely bedridden, and a few months ago I fell into a relationship with another woman. My seven-year-old had been slowly withdrawing from her mother as the sickness grew worse and soon after she died started asking me for another mother. What should I make of this, and how and when should I introduce her to this woman?

Your daughter is telling you that she is lonely for closeness with an adult female. Everyone needs a mother and this is especially true of a little girl. Spending time with women will give her the role models she naturally craves. She also misses the soft touch, the voice, the routines of Mommy. Talk with your child about this yearning: "I know you miss Mommy; what do you miss the most?" You might learn about some things that she needs to have replaced by you or some loving and willing woman. Let her know about other females in her life, aunts, friends, older kids, baby-sitters who can offer her things her own mother gave her. Explain she won't have to do without mothering. Try to make play dates with kids whose mothers will be sensitive to giving her that extra touch. If you can afford it, find a student or woman who can baby-sit a day or two a week so that she can develop a connection with an older girl. Let your daughter know that her desire and need for a mother is normal, of course.

Your daughter is also trying to escape her grief, which is not a good thing to encourage. Sooner or later, the realization that she has lost her own true mother will flood her consciousness. Children at seven are beginning to distinguish between the differences in people. They are discovering that each person possesses particular qualities. They are becoming more skilled in recognizing and developing preferences. She needs to understand that people are not interchangeable but we can love other people for who they are. We can get our needs met both in giving and receiving love. You might get your daughter to talk about the different people she likes and loves and ask her how they are alike and different from one another. "Aunt Ginny bakes cakes with me but Aunt Sue doesn't like to cook so we do our nails when I have a sleepover," she says.

Ask your daughter how she feels about you having a friendship with another woman who could also become her friend? When you feel ready, you can gradually let your daughter know that you have a friend who is a female and that you would like her to meet this person on a particular day. Only make this introduction if you are secure with the friendship part of this relationship. It is important that in the event that you cannot remain lifetime partners, you will be able to work something out so that your daughter is not abruptly abandoned a second time by a woman. Let your daughter know that this woman is a very good friend but not a mommy.

"She can be my mom," your daughter blurts out, "if you get married and then she's my stepmom?"

"What happens to your other mom?" you ask.

Your daughter may look confused and so you may want to talk about how her mom will always be her mom. Reiterate how much her mother loved and was attached to her, maybe how she has Mommy's hair color or musical talent and how this will always be a part of her. She's right, though, if you were to remarry, she would have a stepmom. Another woman to love her.

Include your daughter in your relationship in a measured way. Slowing it down gives everyone a chance to become accustomed to one another and for a dynamic to build and grow.

Maintain a conversation with your daughter about her preferences and perceptions. Ask her questions and share your perceptions. See, hear, or sense her reactions. Honoring her mother and including her memory in all of your lives will allow your child to attach to a new lovable person with less guilt and confusion.

My boyfriend and I break up and get back together and break up and get back together. This is very confusing to my nine- and fourteen-year-old. How should I explain what's going on?

Before you speak to them you need to know why you think it's happening. Are you having trouble meeting each other's needs but neither one of you want to be alone? Do the two of you tend toward a lot of histrionic behaviors? Are these "real" breakups in your mind or do you always know in a week or two things will get back together?

Obviously a pattern of breaking up, coming back together, and breaking up again is not a relationship pattern you will want to model for your children. There are other ways to problem solve within a romance. Don't forget, they've already been through one big breakup that never came back together.

No matter what the reason this separating and coming together is going on, it actually is not necessary to keep your children apprised of every up and down. Certainly you don't need to use words of finality such as "breakup." There are other less frightening terms to draw upon. "Taking a breather." "We need a little space from each other and then we'll see." "Each of us need some time to be alone for a while." These words are without the violence the phrase "breakup" denotes, and also communicate respect for both for yourself and each other.

If it's that you are afraid of being alone again, too much detail isn't a good idea. "I hate not having a boyfriend" teaches dependence at a time when you want your child to learn to stand firm on his own two feet. "I think we're having a bit of trouble figuring out if we're right for each other. Sometimes people can care about each other but not get along that well." This conveys that not any person will do, and that not every breakup means total rejection. This will be a particularly important lesson for your teenager when he or she experiences a broken heart.

If the two of you just tend to be dramatic, flare up easily, and then passionately make up, it would be wise to keep the "scenes" away from your children. When you're not seeing each other simply tell the kids, "We're both swamped right now with other things." Dragging them into your dramas crosses boundaries and may leave them frightened or feeling responsible. "Is there something I should do?" they might think, haunted by their old fears that they did something to bring on the divorce.

Keep in mind the message you are conveying to your children. People in relationships need to treat each other respectfully—not like yo-yos. If you are in a stage of your divorce process in which you simply have not found your balance and this breakup pattern plagues your relationship, then keep the relationship out of the house. Your children need to believe that a stable relationship is possible. They won't understand Mommy or Daddy is trying to find herself or himself. They'll only see your "love" relationships as shaky, undependable, and unhappy experiences. They may believe they won't be capable of anything better.

So if you have to be on a seesaw, try to play in a playground the next town over.

My ten-year-old daughter is very precocious. She always has been. Last night I came home on the early side from a date with my boyfriend because I knew she wasn't crazy about her sitter. Sure enough, she was up and when I went to tuck her into bed she looked up at me with her big brown eyes and asked, "Do you and Steve have sex?"

Depending on your comfort level with your children around the topic of sex, you may need to step back for a moment and collect yourself.

You need to determine how she defines sex. Is she asking in order to find out more about what's going on physically between two adults? Maybe she is asking this question because she really wants to know how serious you and Steve are about this relationship. If he's around a lot and in your bed, chances are you are taking him into your life (and therefore hers). Start with something like, what do you mean when you say "sex"? If she says simple things like kissing and stuff, you can answer that you and Steve like (love) each other and you do kiss and hug because, as she knows, when you really like someone, cuddling and touching feels warm and affectionate and makes you and the other person feel closer and secure. If you have explained sex and sexuality to your daughter, she may not really remember the details. Let her explain what she remembers. Also, this could be a good chance to set it all straight again. It won't be the last time.

You might take this opportunity to ask how she feels about you and Steve being close. She might say fine. If so, you might ask, "What's fine about it? What's not so fine about it?" If she's afraid to say anything "bad," assure her that it's all right with you to feel whatever she feels and then say, "Oh, c'mon, there must be something that you don't like?" If she shrugs, you can tell her, she can let you know if she has any "worries."

The point of this conversation is understanding your daughter's knowledge of closeness and sexuality as well as what her feelings and adjustments are concerning your boyfriend. She may say quite a lot or not much, but this dialogue will give you a future reference point. "Remember when we talked . . . ? Well, I had a thought. . . ." You can then share and ask for her opinion.

If she persists in knowing if you engage in the actual physical act, it's up to you to answer. Some parents may be more comfortable saying something like, "We are very close and show our affections through physical touching." Other parents may feel comfortable saying, "Yes, adults enjoy grown-up ways of expressing their loving feelings, but it is for grown-ups not ten-year-olds." Some parents, however, might simply want to say, "That part of my life is private. Steve and I care about each other a lot and what we do to express that caring is between us. But if you want to know if we hug and kiss and enjoy being close physically, the answer is yes."It's important to normalize adults and their physical relations. It shouldn't be a major mystery or secret because that suggests something is possibly wrong. This might, however, be a good time to remind your daughter of the difference between secrets and privacy.

A guy I've just met and have dated twice called the other day for me. I wasn't home and when my seven-year-old Sammy answered, he engaged him in a conversation about airplanes, something I had mentioned Sammy enjoys. When I arrived home an hour or so later Sammy excitedly reported, "Lester said he'd take me to an airfield that's not far away!" I was infuriated. They hadn't even met, I wasn't sure how I felt about Lester (though now I am), and now I have an excited child on my hands who deserves an explanation.

You will have to let Lester know this kind of behavior is unacceptable. A date should never "enter" your child's life in a manner in which he has clearly not yet been invited. It's unfair to the child (who may read things into this man's interest that cannot possibly be true) and to you (who will be left holding the bag).

"Sammy, you know how sometimes you are nice to someone and then all of a sudden they think they're you're best friend— like that time you gave Timmy his homework assignment and then he called you every day and you never really thought he was so much fun? Honestly, that's kind of how I feel about Lester. He's a guy I went out with just two times and I think he thought we were going to be great friends. But the truth is I don't like him that much and I don't especially want to see him again, and I certainly don't think it's right for him to take you to the airfield."

Timmy may balk. "But I want to go!! He sounded nice!"

In a way, Timmy has been victimized by your dating life. It would be important here to work out something positive for Timmy, quickly. You don't want him to assume you date a bunch of jerks.

"I'll tell you what. I'll ask your uncle and cousin if they want to track down that airfield and we can all go some Sunday afternoon soon! You can bring your new camera so we can remember everything we saw. It will be great!"

Timmy will likely jump at this. (It's smart to think of a male figure to accompany you because that was the dynamic Timmy might have also had in mind.)

Then add something like, "Lester shouldn't have asked you without asking me first. He didn't mean any harm."

On my son's twelfth birthday he got a new mountain bike and the news that I was leaving his mother. The marriage was dead eight years ago when my daughter left for college but I suffered and stayed for my son's sake until I couldn't any longer. His mother has him brainwashed to believe that she had no idea we were in trouble and I up and abandoned her. She cries to my son and overwhelms him and then he comes to us for a weekend visit prepared to hate my partner. How do I set this straight without trashing his mother's behavior?

You have to let your son know that you and your mother see things very differently but that he does not have to take sides. Acknowledge that his mother sees you as the bad guy. You know that she is very upset and hurt that the marriage didn't work out and it's easy to make one person the villain. Over time, you are hoping perspectives will change. Let him see how difficult this must be for him.

"Guess you are feeling in the middle, huh?"

"You shouldn't have left Mom for someone else." He shrugs with a tight, angry gaze.

"I left because Mom and I grew apart, we just couldn't feel really the way we felt when we had you. Not every love has to change but ours did. After our love changed I met Theresa. Theresa didn't ruin our marriage. It had already fallen apart."

"What's the difference," your son says. "Mom says a vow is forever." Jay's eyes well up.

"When I made my vow, I did want it to be and believed it would be forever but in this case, we weren't satisfied and even though Mom would have stayed under any circumstances, she was feeling unhappy and hurt too."

"She cries to me all the time."

"Any marriage ending is sad and Mom, well, feels like crying a lot. It's hard for her not to let you see that even though it is tough on you. It is very difficult for children to see their mother unhappy." You might say that you knew a girl in the same circumstance who felt helpless and depressed and at a loss about how to help her mother who seemed inconsolable like Mom. This gives Jay some way to recognize his feelings at a distance. Remember, he is a near teen and may not want to say so much to you about his tender and vulnerable feelings. Also, he may feel that to say more would be to betray his mother. If he does want to air emotion, he may say, "I feel that way sometimes," or something a bit more protective like, "Oh yeah, what did she do?" Here you could offer that she decided to find someone to talk to because she felt so burdened by her mother. She went to a counselor at school for advice. It helped her not feel guilty and isolated. Depending on the vibe you get either in his expression or verbal response, you could offer to help him find one for himself.

It is critical not to devalue his mother. Let him know that your concern is that he can feel free to like who he wants to like and love who he wants to love. That he knows that when someone, anyone, not just Mom, though she is the one having a hard time now, is going through so much pain, the people around them cannot take the pain away. That person has to work on healing himself or herself.

Don't be surprised to get a small amount of feedback from Jay; teens can be exceedingly private. He has heard you, however. You will do best to get these issues opened up and across to him without judging anyone's behavior. It is what it is and your goal is finding any healthy way to move it along.

In the meantime, if there is any way to get your wife to seek help and have a place to bring her sorrow rather than venting and involving your child, it would be enormously beneficial to your son. Perhaps there is someone the two of you know in common who would be willing to suggest this to her.

I separated from my wife of twenty-eight years about eleven months ago. It was hell. On a job this summer, I met a woman who became a friend and very recently it turned romantic. My kids are twenty-eight and thirty and I figured it was no big deal to bring her to a holiday gathering at the home of my oldest daughter, who is married with one little girl. I haven't spoken much to my children about the divorce. I've just said that I'm doing okay. At the party, one daughter was cold and curt to my date. My ex managed to be more cordial. Both my girls are close to their mother and I don't know how to handle this exactly but I feel lousy. They stuck by her side the whole time.

It's not easy to put one's needs aside in circumstances such as these, but it's important to at least lay them out on the table—in this case beforehand, in order to make a wise decision.

The problem started before the party. You and your daughters need to sit down and talk about the feelings you are all having about this change. Even adult children hold on to the idea that their parents will be getting back together again. At the very least they can be extraordinarily protective of the spouse who was "left." Your attending a party with another woman, with no warning, in front of your entire family, may have been just too much of a jolt to everyone.

You might call your daughter and say, "I know this ending between your mother and myself is upsetting for you and I don't want you to feel as bad as you do."

"Then why put it in my face in front of my friends, my mother, and Aunt Lily?"

You're only real choice is to be direct. "I know it makes you feel the sadness and anger about Mom and I having split up, but I have made other friends," can acknowledge your daughter's feelings while at the same time stating your need.

"I have to admit I was really only thinking of what would make me happy. I didn't consider how all of you would feel." Then you might add the divorce has been hard for you too. "I've been very lonely. I'm used to a marriage and just because it didn't last for a lifetime with your mother, it doesn't mean I have to be alone."

Don't be surprised if the sistership thing appears like a bolt from the blue. "I'm so mad at you for leaving Mom, she's an older woman and she's alone! It's so selfish." She's right. It does tend to be harder for women. Maybe she feels burdened by her mother not doing very well and feels you should have stood by her no matter what you needed.

Again, you'll need to address the truth. "I'm sorry your mother is having a hard time too. I wish it were easier. I still care about her very much. We tried the best we both could to make the marriage last but we couldn't. But as upset as you feel, we all have to go on. You and your sister have your own lives and I have to build mine."

Finally, you might consider an alternate plan for family gatherings. If it's too soon and your daughter(s) needs more time to adjust, you could consider backing off on dating in front of the family until more time passes. If you are able, you can speak these feelings out loud with your daughter. This particular party might have been a blessing in disguise. Painful though it was, it did get you communicating.

My twelve-year-old daughter, Lucy, is still talking about her dad and I getting back together someday. My ex and I have managed to cooperate with each other around parenting surprisingly well, but there is no chance that we will ever remarry and I have explained that to my daughter as gently as I could. So on Friday night I was at a loss. Her dad was coming to pick her up for the weekend and I had a date. Both my ex and I arrived at my house within five minutes of one another to find a beautiful, really exceptional meal that she had made laid out for the two of us (with the help of an innocent teen baby-sitter), candlelight and all. I almost started to cry, but instead snapped she should have asked first. Needless to say she ran from the room in tears. What might I have done?

There was no way your child could have escaped this situation unscathed. The dinner represented her most cherished wish and you had to not only reject that dream but also render her efforts something of a failure.

The first thing to consider is whether the message of the finality of your divorce has gotten through to her from *both* parents. Has your ex been as adamant as you? A slight perceived uncertainty will allow your child to run with the ball. It's a good idea to discuss this in detail with your ex, so that nothing like this happens again.

Complimenting your daughter on her ability to prepare such a wonderful meal and expressing your pride would go a long way to at least acknowledging her supreme culinary abilities and maturity. You'll then want to move to the bad news, which is twofold. One, you won't be there to eat it because you're going out, and two, you and your ex no longer dine together like this because you are no longer married.

"Oh, a date?" your daughter sneers.

"Yes, I have a date tonight like I often do on Fridays as you know."

"I thought you might want to stay if I made a great dinner for both of you." Lucy's lower lip trembles.

Now is the time to be straight with her. If necessary and if possible you might want to call your date and change your plans and suggest to your ex that he hang out to talk a bit before taking Lucy for the evening. Both you and your ex know that there will be no reconciliation and perhaps both of you telling her once again, calmly but clearly together, will bring the facts "home."

"Lucy, Dad and I love you dearly and we loved each other in that very special way when we had you but our love for each other is a friendship love now and that means we can't be romantic anymore even though you made a lovely and romantic dinner for us."

"But why? You loved each other once, you could again, couldn't you?"

You know Lucy desperately wants to hold on to her notion of your reconciliation and being faced head-on with her own helplessness to make things come out that way is an emotional injury for her. It can bruise her sense of power or control. You or your ex might want to say something like, "You have been able to motivate Dad and I to have the best friendship we can have. We do this because of you and what you mean to us but even though this is hard for you and painful, we are not going to be a couple like we used to be. Only friends. I'm sorry, I know this hurts you. Sometimes feelings between adults go from one kind of love to another. A parent's love for children never changes, but between a man and a woman sometimes it can."

The truth is somewhere in her heart and mind Lucy probably knew what the outcome of her efforts would be. Children will often put aside what they deeply know in favor of that for which they most deeply wish. Keep in mind that no matter how distressed Lucy appeared, part of this might have been the outpouring of sadness she already had stored deep within, which no longer had an excuse to stay underground.

Finally, you might want to ask Lucy to save you some of the food so that you can enjoy what she has made. Maybe you can taste some and have a light snack before you go off for the evening. Your ex and Lucy can decide if they want to eat together.

There's no escaping a child's wish to keep parents together. All you can do is state the truth as clearly as you can, making sure to emphasize that you will all still be a part of each other's lives and that the love you and her dad feel for her will never, ever go away.

> I adopted a child on my own because I waited and waited to find a partner and it just never happened. I always thought I would date but with the demands of single parenting, I rarely get time to meet and develop anything with adults. My daughter, Cami, is seven now and yesterday said, "Mommy, when I get a husband, do you want to share him?" I laughed and then didn't really know what to say.

Cami is giving you an opening to talk about partnership and romantic love. At her age girls and boys become quite aware of the different genders. Children also have questions about where they come from and it's important to give them the message that they are free to ask. Truthfulness in an appropriate proportion is very important. Secrets tend to make children's imaginations run wild.

Assuming she knows something about the way she came to exist and has seemed satisfied for the time being, you might ask Cami why she thinks she needs a husband or if she thinks you do.

"Everyone at school has a husband," she says.

"Really, you mean a dad?" Cami nods and tells you that there are lots of dads who play with the children.

Cami is probably wondering about where your husband and her dad is. Even though she may have some information, this may be a time when it's important to give a little more. If he was a friend, why is he not around now? If she was adopted from another country you might postulate where her birth father might be. More complex explanations for, as an example, artificial insemination may require consultations with specialists so that her specific questions can be answered in a helpful, healthy way.

You need to formulate something that you feel comfortable telling her about how she came to be.

Cami may be wondering why there is no man in either of your lives. If you are interested in companionship but have had no time, you can tell her that you would like a friend who is a man who might also become her friend but that you have been very busy being a mother and working. "I wish I could find the right guy to be with us but I just haven't yet. I'm hoping I will though."

"I don't see you trying," she might say. "Nobody calls for dates."

You can put her off with a "Let me think about that . . ." if you're not sure. If you discover after some self-exploration that you've been purposefully hiding, you might say, "You know, honey, I was thinking about what you said about me and guys. I think I really haven't been trying to meet anyone and I might just get out there more now and look around!" If you realize you simply don't want a partner, you can say, "Sometimes adults prefer to be on their own. We certainly don't need a man to take care of us. I can do that! But I think you're telling me that you would like to have a 'guy' around more. Maybe we can ask Uncle Tim to do some stuff with us at school or maybe even go on a class trip with you!" In other words, you might bring into her consciousness the availability of other men in her life.

It might also be interesting to explore what Cami is seeking in her desire to share a husband with you. Does she see a man as someone who takes care of a mommy and little girl? Clearly, a child is influenced by what she observes at school and in movies and television. If a close friend or relative has an intact family, she may simply enjoy certain aspects of that family constellation. She may be trying to tell you how badly she would like a daddy. For Cami and for you, getting easy and comfortable with your own family configuration is key. But this may require you making an effort to more actively integrate male friends and relatives into your lives to satisfy your daughter's need for a male figure to be consistently in her life.